BRANCH LINES AROUND HUNTINGDON

KETTERING TO CAMBRIDGE

Vic Mitchell   Keith Smith
Christopher Awdry   Allan Mott

First published June 1991
Reprinted July 1993

ISBN 0 906520 93 2

© *Middleton Press 1991*

Design - Deborah Goodridge

Published by Middleton Press
        Easebourne Lane
        Midhurst
        West Sussex
        Tel: (0730) 813169

Printed & bound by Biddles Ltd,
        Guildford and Kings Lynn

CONTENTS

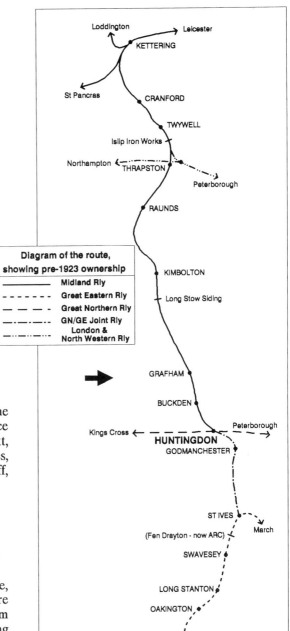

Diagram of the route, showing pre-1923 ownership

————————— Midland Rly
- - - - - - - - Great Eastern Rly
— — — — — Great Northern Rly
—.—.—.—.— GN/GE Joint Rly
—..—..—..— London & North Western Rly

ACKNOWLEDGEMENTS

In addition to those mentioned in the captions, we are very grateful for the assistance received from R.I.Burn-Murdoch, R.Butt, K.Gilbert, P.Hay, D.Hufford, Miss L.S.James, K.Loughlin, D.Salter, P.C.Saunders, E.Staff, N.Stanyon, Prof. H.P. White and our wives.

GEOGRAPHICAL SETTING

The line served an area, rich in iron ore, between Kettering and Thrapston, before crossing the River Nene. It then climbed from the valley and crossed the gently rolling agricultural upland of London Clay between the Rivers Nene and Ouse. Descending to the Ouse near Huntingdon, it followed that river before finally taking to the rich, flat lands to the south of the Fens and, after joining the line from Ely at Chesterton Junction, ran into Cambridge from the north.

The maps are to the scale of 25" to 1 mile, unless otherwise stated.

HISTORICAL BACKGROUND

The first north-south main line in the area opened between London and Birmingham in 1838 and became part of the London and North Western Railway. Next came the London to Cambridge line in 1845, part of the Great Eastern Railway for most of its early years. The Great Northern Railway's route between London (Kings Cross) and Peterborough via Huntingdon was completed in 1850. Finally part of the Midland Railway's main line came into use in 1857, between Hitchin and Leicester.

After several early attempts to build railways in the ironstone region east of Kettering, a line from Kettering to Huntingdon was projected in two stages in 1860. The first part, the Kettering & Thrapstone (sic) Railway received its authorising Act on 29th July 1862, having gone through Parliament very smoothly compared with other projects of the period. Even before this section was open, plans were afoot for the Huntingdon extension, and again the Bill met little opposition - the Kettering, Thrapstone & Huntingdon Railway was sanctioned on 28th July 1863, the Act providing for working by the MR at a rate of 40% of the gross receipts for the first seven years, and at 50% thereafter. Progress with building was good, though excessive haste may have led to the deaths of at least two navvies, when, in separate incidents, they were overwhelmed by earthfalls. The Board of Trade inspector approved the line between Kettering and Huntingdon on 15th February 1866, the first goods train ran six days later, and passenger traffic began on 1st March, when, on a bitterly cold day, many went to their local station to watch the first train. Huntingdon had been approached from the east by the Lynn & Ely Railway, which projected an extension of its line from Ely to St.Ives, and this was opened on 17th August 1847. It was worked at first by the Eastern Counties Railway, but for a short time (from 1st October to 31st December 1849) the East Anglian Railways (now owners of the L&E) worked a horse-tram service on the line. The ECR resumed operation on 1st January 1850 and, in 1862, the Great Eastern Railway took over. This section later became part of the GN/GE Joint Railway under an Act of 1879.

The line between St.Ives and Cambridge, although projected by the Wisbech, St.Ives & Cambridge Railway, was actually built by the ECR and opened on the same day as the L&E section, becoming GER property in due course.

Results on the Midland section did not reach the expectations of the prospectus. After initial enthusiasm the passenger receipts dropped until the first timetable was revised, although the Duke of Manchester, who owned much of the land through which the line passed, was less than pleased with the new schedule.

After the 1923 Grouping, the London, Midland & Scottish took control west of Huntingdon and the London & North Eastern Railway eastwards. Soon the ironstone at the western end of the line became exhausted, and this, together with the increase in motor transport, caused a decline in the line's importance. World War II increased traffic when essential materials, bombs and ammunition were carried to a US Air Force base at Stow Longa. Twywell closed in 1951 and Cranford five years later. A viability study carried out on the route between Kettering and Huntingdon in 1958 showed that things were not as they should be, and in 1959 BR announced closure. Despite objections, passenger services ceased from 15th June of that year. The final train had run on the previous Saturday, 13th June, since there was no Sunday service. For no apparent reason the track was maintained however, though hopes of a revival came to nothing. On 15th June 1959, the Huntingdon-St.Ives section closed. The ten miles of track between Kimbolton and Huntingdon and between St. Ives and Godmanchester were lifted in June 1961. What remained at the Kettering end was used for crew-training in August 1962. After the severe winter of 1962-63, during which a bridge near Raunds collapsed, it was no great shock when BR announced that all traffic would cease from 28th October 1963, except the Twywell ore trains. These continued until 20th January 1978.

The St.Ives-Cambridge section fared better. Passenger trains continued until 5th October 1970, and the line remains open as far as Fen Drayton, to serve gravel pits there. Recent efforts by the Railway Development Society to promote a reopening for passengers remain unrealised.

1. On the opening day, 7th August 1850, the first train to pass north through Huntingdon conveyed "a party of about 400 gentlemen in some 17 carriages".

PASSENGER SERVICES

To begin with, there were four passenger trains each way (two on Sundays), the all-stations journey of 47¾ miles taking two hours. One faster train each way, (leaving Kettering at 11.30am and Cambridge at 11.05am) took 20 minutes less westbound and 35 minutes less eastbound. By 1887 the Sunday service had been discontinued, though the weekday pattern remained similar. The fast train now left Kettering at 3.30pm, taking 1 hour 50 minutes for its journey - the balancing trip had left Cambridge at 11.30am, reaching its destination at 1.07pm. In 1906 five trains left Kettering on weekdays, though one, leaving at 11.30am, ran only to Thrapston, and the last (departing at 4.00pm) terminated at Godmanchester. The fast train, leaving at 2.25pm, reached Cambridge in just under an hour and a half, at 3.54: the 2.50pm in the other direction took an hour and 25 minutes. There were more Kettering departures in 1914, but still only four through trains to Cambridge. There was also a rather curious Tuesdays-only working between Thrapston and Kimbolton for which there seems to have been no return working.

By 1925 the service had been slowed and reduced, the fast service leaving Kettering at 10.35 and taking 1 hour 37 minutes to reach Cambridge - the opposite working, leaving Cambridge at 11.35, took 1 hour 40 minutes. The pattern had changed little by 1938. The fast train, leaving Kettering 14 minutes later, took just one minute longer to complete the journey than it had 13 years before.

In the years just after World War II, heavy holiday trains, often double-headed, would use the line to wend their way slowly towards East Coast resorts. Hot, overcrowded compartments can have been no pleasurable start to a holiday. Under BR management there were fewer all-stations trains, all taking slightly under two hours, but there were still only four trains each way. In the last year of operation of the complete route there were only three local trains each way, plus a Clacton-Leicester service in the summer months.

In 1901, Kettering had many more facilities than it boasts now, though the station itself is largely intact and retains much Midland atmosphere. The locomotive shed has completely gone, and the site of the engine shed and other facilities are now a car park. To the south the beginning of the branch to Cransley Ironworks and Loddington can be seen curving westward - it was taken out of use on 1st October 1980. Though the goods shed and other buildings still stand, on the up side, the track layout has been simplified beyond recognition. The scale is 6 inches to 1 mile.

KETTERING

2. Two additional platforms came into use on 10th August 1879, but the main line quadrupling was not completed until 1884. Deeley Compound 4-4-0 no. 1006 arrives at Kettering with an afternoon down train, 3rd September 1933. The first carriage is a 48ft brake third of 1902. Note the splendid gas-lamps, alas no longer with us. (H.C.Casserley)

3. Johnson Class 1P 2-4-0 no. 194 stands at Kettering's island platform on a Cambridge train on 26th June 1934. The engine has undergone some modification since building, having gained a Belpaire firebox but lost its original smokebox, dome cover, and perhaps most sadly of all, its shapely brass safety valve cover. The first carriage looks of a similar vintage to that in the picture above. (V. Webster)

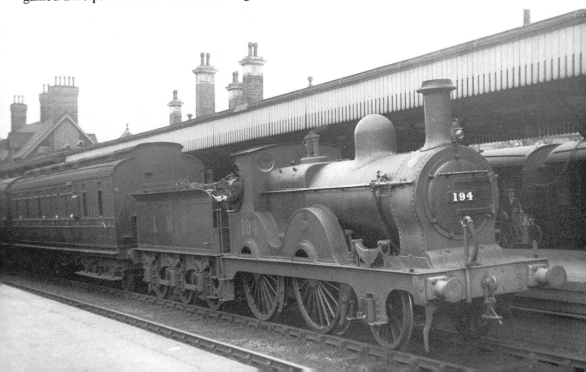

4. Another modified Johnson 2-4-0, this time no. 266, shunts coaches for a Cambridge train in Kettering yard on 26th June 1934. The carriage is a comparatively recent LMS brake 3rd of 1930 - several of the type were converted to motor driving vehicle, the equivalent of the GWR auto-trailers. (V. Webster)

6. Kettering is seen in 1990, looking south, as a DMU is about to leave at 19.00 for Bletchley, via Bedford. Note the distinctive Midland canopy cheek by jowl - and by no means suffering in the comparison - with colour-light signalling and state-of-the-art wastebins. (A.Mott)

5. Johnson 2-4-0 no. 207 and 0-6-0 no. 3564 prepare to leave Kettering with a Cambridge train on 26th June 1934. The first coach here is no. 236, a lavatory/third/brake composite, built at the turn of the century. (V. Webster)

7. The facade at Kettering survives, if much else has gone. A Midland canopy still performs its original function, and the MR monogram still decorates the gable to the left. How many of BR's stations have got one of those...? (A.Mott)

8. Fine and functional, or simply functional - seeing the two side by side, readers will no doubt make their own judgement. The station was rebuilt in 1879-84 and further alterations took place in 1896. The train service to Corby was withdrawn in 1966 but reinstated from 11th May 1987 until 4th June 1990. (A.Mott)

KETTERING SHED

9. 3rd September 1933 was a Sunday, and this is borne out by the generous locomotive line-up, (there are a brakevan and an open wagon in there too) combined with the fact that there seems to be a shed-visit in progress. The depot opened in 1865. (H.C.Casserley)

10. Kirtley double-framed 2-4-0 is seen on 26th June 1934 as LMS no. 20012. There were 29 of these locomotives, introduced in 1866 - they had a long and useful life, the last one surviving in service until 1947. It is now part of the National Collection, and as no. 158A can be seen at the Midland Railway Centre, Butterley. (V.Webster)

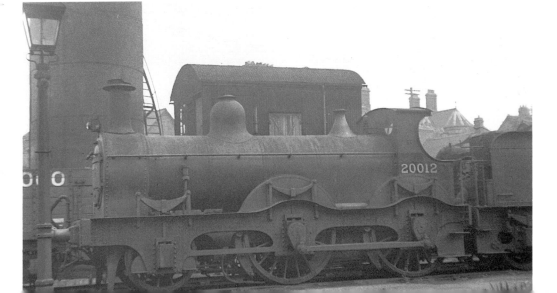

11. Seen just after nationalisation, no. 23011 is being coaled up on 7th July 1948. Loaded wagons were propelled up the ramp; the coal was shovelled out onto a steel platform and then loaded into wheeled tubs which were manhandled to the coaling doorway.
(H.C.Casserley)

12. This cab-view of Johnson 2-4-0, ex-MR and now LMS no. 20216 looks north from the shed on 10th August 1945. Kettering North signalbox can be glimpsed beyond the parapets of the bridge spanning Kettering's Northampton Road. This box was in use from 1898 until November 1967, when South Box also closed. Station Box remained functional until 5th December 1987. (H.C.Casserley)

13. On 1st September 1954, the shed appears quiet. No.46444 on the left was one of the mainstays of the Kettering-Cambridge line, and we shall meet it again. Standard Class 2 Mogul no. 78021 was only four months old at this date, and almost certainly saw service on the branch too. The shed closed on 14th June 1965. (V.Webster)

KETTERING JUNCTION

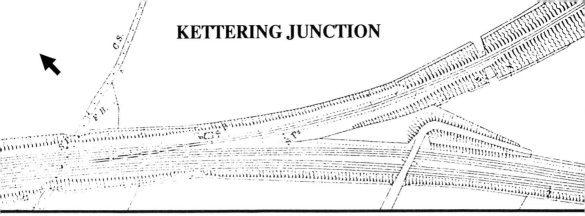

The Cambridge branch parted from the main line at Kettering Junction, and trains for the branch left via a fifth road beside the main line. Trains coming off the branch at first crossed to the down slow at Pytchley, which was the tablet point. Later, trains for Kettering could leave the branch via the up line at Kettering Junction and use a crossover to the down slow. Wicksteed Park, a popular 100-acre leisure centre opened in 1921, partly occupies the upper part of the map. Norman Marlow, a University lecturer, did duties at Kettering Junction signal box during vacations, and has left a fascinating account in his book *Footplate and Signal Cabin* (Allen & Unwin, 1956).

14. A Cambridge train climbs away from Kettering Junction on 26th June 1934, headed by Johnson 2-4-0 no. 225, with a mixed rake of LMS and turn-of-the-century Midland stock, and what looks like a cattle wagon bringing up the rear. The telegraph poles behind the embankment are beside the main line. (V.Webster)

15. Before turning east, the branch had to skirt Wicksteed Park. When this 1969 picture of the Park's well-filled miniature train was taken, the passenger service on the Kettering to Cambridge branch was already sinking into history. (A.Mott)

CRANFORD

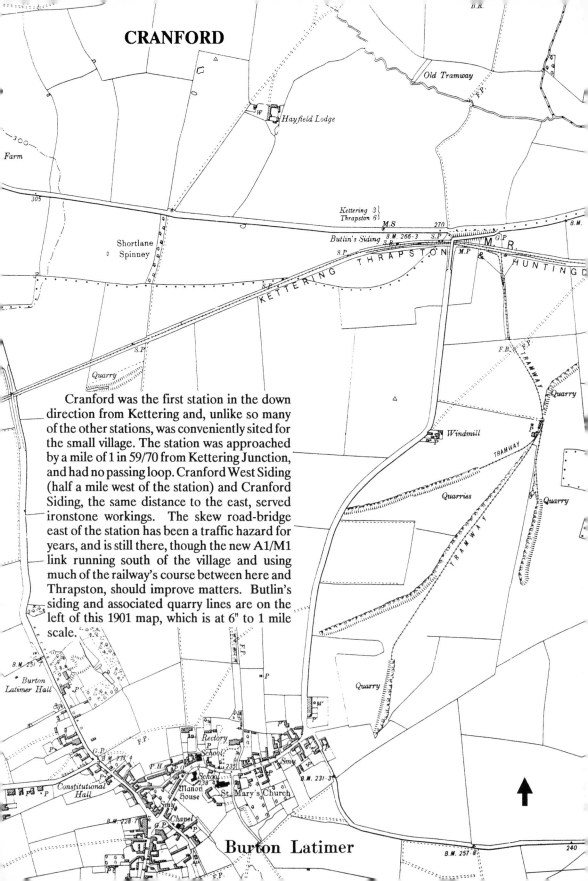

Cranford was the first station in the down direction from Kettering and, unlike so many of the other stations, was conveniently sited for the small village. The station was approached by a mile of 1 in 59/70 from Kettering Junction, and had no passing loop. Cranford West Siding (half a mile west of the station) and Cranford Siding, the same distance to the east, served ironstone workings. The skew road-bridge east of the station has been a traffic hazard for years, and is still there, though the new A1/M1 link running south of the village and using much of the railway's course between here and Thrapston, should improve matters. Butlin's siding and associated quarry lines are on the left of this 1901 map, which is at 6" to 1 mile scale.

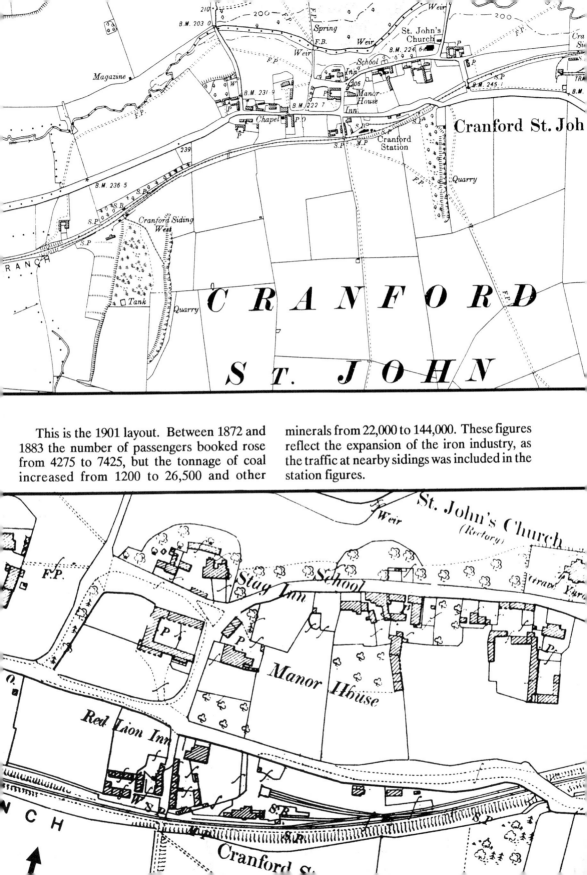

This is the 1901 layout. Between 1872 and 1883 the number of passengers booked rose from 4275 to 7425, but the tonnage of coal increased from 1200 to 26,500 and other minerals from 22,000 to 144,000. These figures reflect the expansion of the iron industry, as the traffic at nearby sidings was included in the station figures.

16. The attractive-looking station, built of local stone, was opened for goods on 21st February 1866 and for passengers on 1st March the same year. This undated picture seems so timeless it might have been taken at any time since then. The notorious skew bridge can just be glimpsed in the background, and the signalpost visible to the right of the line, beyond the station signalbox, is tall enough for the arm to be seen above the bridge by enginemen. (D.Tack)

17. After just over 90 years of service to passengers, Cranford station was closed to them on 2nd April 1956. It remained open for goods until 6th November 1961 and was then sold as a private dwelling. Both platform and building remain largely intact and retain their charm. (A.Mott)

TWYWELL

18. After its sharp rise to Cranford the line fell towards Twywell at 1 in 93/70/200. The station, half a mile from the village it served, never boasted a long platform, which, no doubt because of the site, was built on the side of the line remote from the village, and there was no crossing loop. The station's opening dates are the same as those of Cranford, but closure for both passenger and goods traffic came on 30th July 1951. The signalbox remained usable until 30th August 1953. (D.Thompson)

19. Since closure much has changed under private ownership. The main part of the station building seems intact (even the ridge retains its slightly concave profile), but extension work has been done and the station yard looked a good deal tidier when this picture was taken on 7th July 1990 than it had done some 35 years before. (A.Mott)

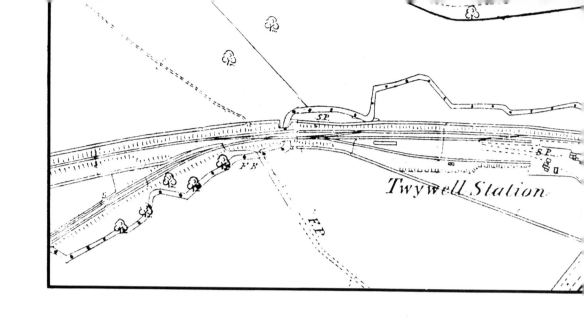

Twywell Station

ISLIP FURNACES

Half a mile east of Twywell station the line fanned into a substantial complex to serve the Islip Furnaces. The A1/M1 link has obliterated the course of the railway here, and any re- maining traces of a tramway which led south to Newbridge Quarry. This had an internal system gauged at 2ft 3in, and closed in 1922.

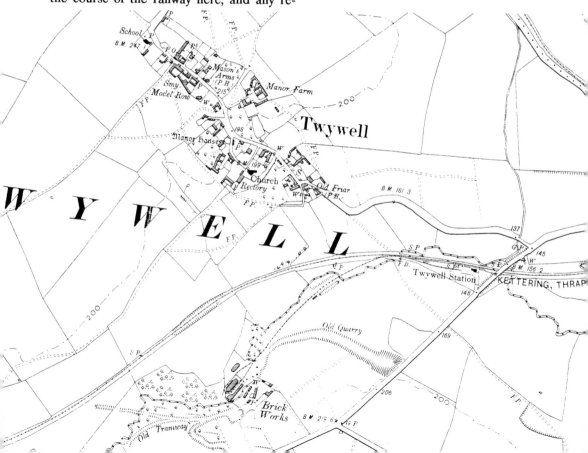

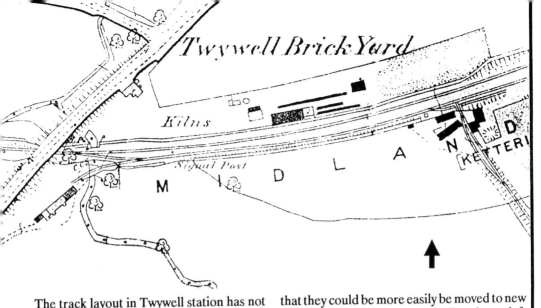

The track layout in Twywell station has not altered much across the years. The same cannot be said of the area on either side of the station, for ironstone lines were lightly built so that they could be more easily be moved to new or extended ore workings. The lines lower left and lower right were both associated with brickworks marked on this 1st edition.

Islip's main source of ore was from extensive quarries to the north, which had the largest narrow-gauge system in the ironstone industry - 2ft 6in gauge in the adits themselves and 3ft between them and the furnaces. This is the 2nd edition of 1901 at 6" to 1 mile.

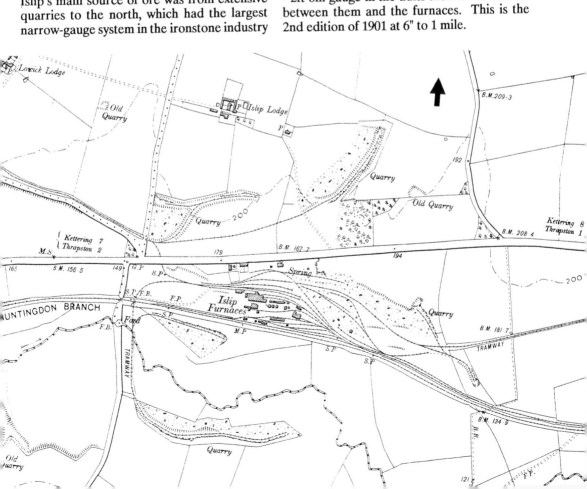

20. This view shows Islip Furnaces from the south, across the shallow valley of the stream, seen in the foreground, which flows eastwards to join the River Nene some two miles away, near Thrapston. The quarries lay beyond the ridge, and the 3ft gauge access line burrowed beneath the old A604 road behind the trees to the left of the buildings. The last load came down from the quarries on 25th October 1952. (J.A.Peden)

21. As well as the 3ft gauge railway system inside the Islip site, there were independent standard gauge connections to the Midland line here, and to the L&NWR at Thrapston. In this picture, narrow-gauge 0-4-0 ST no. 11 *Dike* stands outside its shed in July 1949, with another, larger, locomotive beyond. *Dike* was built by Hudswell Clarke (W/N 1452) in 1921, and came to Islip from Finedon Quarries. It was scrapped in 1953.
(Industrial Railway Society/K J Cooper Coll.)

22. One of the standard gauge engines, Peckett 0-6-0ST *Betty*, (W/N 1549) was photographed during July 1949. Built in 1919 for the Bloxham & Whiston Ironstone Co., she came to Islip in 1931, and moved on to Buckminster mines in December 1952.
(Industrial Railway Society/K J Cooper Coll.)

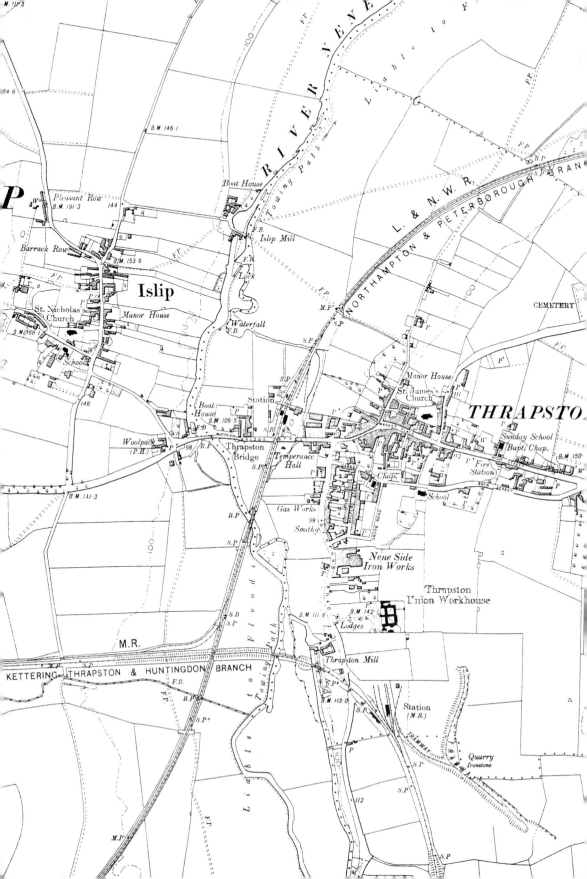

THRAPSTON

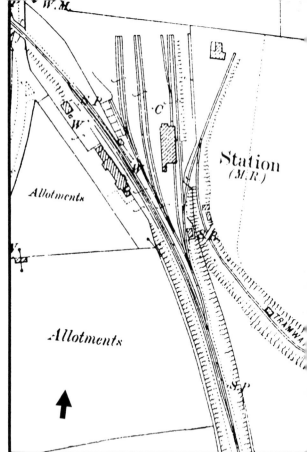

At Thrapston, the first station since Kettering where two trains could be crossed, the line swung southwards, having crossed the LNWR Northampton - Peterborough line (opened 2nd June 1845), the River Nene and a Nene overflow channel on two viaducts. Another bridge across the road to Raunds led into the station itself. A goods yard served an ironstone quarry east of the station, a narrow gauge tramway linking the two. West of the river, a spur linked the line with the LNWR branch. This six inch scale map is from 1901.

23. The lady's costume would suggest that this picture was taken at about the turn of the century, while a Kettering-bound train leaves Thrapston station. It is about to cross the old, not-too-solid-looking viaduct, replaced in 1920 by a blue-brick structure, parts of which can be seen today. (Lens of Sutton)

The station area is shown at 25" to 1 mile.

24. The first station here, called Thrapstone, opened for goods on 21st February 1866 and for passengers on 1st March. The "E" was dropped from the name, seemingly around October 1885, and it became Thrapston Midland Road on 2nd June 1924, to distinguish it from the former LNWR station (Bridge Street), nearer the town centre. A glimpse of the goods yard can be seen to the right, and behind the up platform shelter is the cattle-dock. The picture was taken in the early 1950s. (Lens of Sutton)

25. Looking the other way, an MR signalbox, opened on 3rd February 1892, guards the entrance to the goods yard. Beyond, the track curves southwards and begins a stiff 2-mile climb at 1 in 80. (Lens of Sutton)

26. The colonnaded waiting shelter on the down side at Thrapston is seen on 1st September 1954. In the couple of years or so since the previous two pictures were taken the globe gas-lamps have been replaced by lamps of a more modern pattern. (V.Webster)

27. LNER Class J15 0-6-0 no. 65457 comes off Bridge 23 (the road underbridge) and into Thrapston station on 18th July 1958, with a Cambridge train. This maintained the line's tradition of ancient motive power, for this type had been introduced to the GER by Wilson Worsdell in 1883. (R.M.Casserley)

28. Thrapston station closed to passengers on 15th June 1959, and for goods on 28th October 1963. By 12th September 1990, though still recognisable as a one-time station, it looked very different from its railway days. (A.Mott)

29. The view westward across the Nene Valley from Thrapston station site in 1990, shows contractors putting in a section of the A1/M1 link. Remains of the 1920 viaduct can be seen on the extreme right. (A.Mott)

RAUNDS

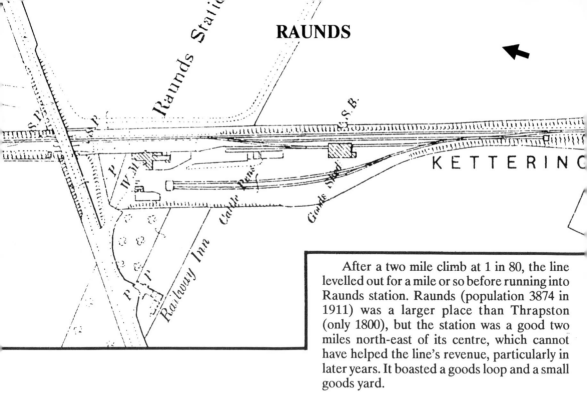

After a two mile climb at 1 in 80, the line levelled out for a mile or so before running into Raunds station. Raunds (population 3874 in 1911) was a larger place than Thrapston (only 1800), but the station was a good two miles north-east of its centre, which cannot have helped the line's revenue, particularly in later years. It boasted a goods loop and a small goods yard.

30. A train for Kettering was expected when this picture was taken on 8th July 1958, as a man waits with his dog. The signalbox, a replacement, can be seen opposite the goods shed, and was opened on 29th July 1891. (R.M.Casserley)

31. In this view of the station, taken from the other side ten days later, the same well-kept van is parked in almost the same place. Staff transport, one might suggest. In the early 1880s, the annual returns for this station showed about 6000 passengers booked, around 80 trucks of cattle handled, over 3000 tons of coal unloaded and nearly 2000 tons of other minerals in or out. (R.M.Casserley)

32. Here is the same place from the same angle, but 32 years intervene. Not a great deal has changed other than an extension of what was previously the reception area. The station's opening and closing dates are identical with those of Thrapston. (A.Mott)

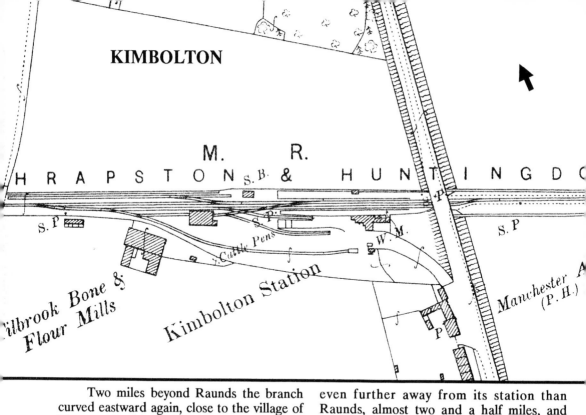

KIMBOLTON

M. R.

HRAPSTON S.B. & HUNTINGDO

S. P.

S. P.

S. P.

S. P.

Cattle Pens

W. M.

ilbrook Bone &
Flour Mills

Kimbolton Station

Manchester A
(P. H.)

Two miles beyond Raunds the branch curved eastward again, close to the village of Hargrave, which did not rate a station, presumably because there was no road access between village and railway. Another three miles brought the line to Kimbolton, which was

even further away from its station than Raunds, almost two and a half miles, and nearer, in fact, to the village of Catworth. The layout was not dissimilar to that at Raunds, but faced Kettering rather than Cambridge, and there were two tracks through the station.

33. Kimbolton opened for goods traffic on 21st February 1866 and for passengers on 1st March. The station building on the south, or down, side of the line was identical with that at Raunds. This pre-WWII view looking towards Cambridge does not show the gravel siding

installed for the wartime airfield at Stow Longa. It ran off to the left, beyond the bridge, at an angle of about 30 degrees. The points faced Cambridge, and the siding ran back as far as the road. In 1960 a Blue Pullman spent some time here. (Lens of Sutton)

34. Johnson class 3F 0-6-0 no. 3195 is seen between bridges 41 and 42, approaching Kimbolton, with a Cambridge train on 22nd July 1939. The coaches are of LMS vintage, the leading vehicle a Stanier corridor brake composite, but the rest looks older. (H.C.Casserley)

35. In this view looking west, the station building's bay window is on the left, and at the end of the down platform is the timber signalbox. This opened on 29th November 1891, replacing a pre-1876 box, and lasted out the life of the branch. In the mid 1870s, around 10,000 passengers were booked annually, along with 150 cattle trucks, 3500 tons of coal and 1500 tons of minerals. (Lens of Sutton)

KETTERING, HUNTINGDON, and CAMBRIDGE.—L. M. & S.

Miles from Kettering.	Down.	Week Days only.							
	Central Station,	ngt.	mrn	mrn		aft.	aft		
	547 Liverpool....dep.	10 L45	5 5	8 30	....	1255	3a30	....	....
	547 M'chester (Cen) "	12 L0	7 20	9 55	....	1 45	4a35	....	....
	605 Birmingham A "	mrn	7 30	1148	....	1 52	4 55	....	....
	547 Derby .... "	6 36	8 51	12 0	....	3 30	6b4	....	....
	547 Leicester (L.R.) "	7 51	9 44	1 5	....	4 15	6 47	....	....
	536 London (St. P.) "	4 25	8 25	1135	....	3 30	6 25	....	....
—	Kettering ....dep.	8 33	1035	2 18	....	5 7	7 58	....	....
4¼	Cranford	8 44	1046	2 29	....	5 18	8 12	....	....
7	Twywell	8 49	1051	2 34	....	5 23	8 17	....	....
9¼	Thrapston B 363 ..	8 55	1057	2 40	....	5 27	8 23	....	....
12¼	Raunds	9 5	11 6	2 50	....	....	8 32	....	....
17¼	Kimbolton C	9 15	1115	3 0	....	....	8 42	....	....
22¼	Grafham	9 23	1124	3 9	....	....	8 50	....	....
25	Buckden	9 29	1130	3 15	....	....	8 56	....	....
27½	Huntingdon 688, 695	9 36	1136	3 22	....	....	9 3	....	....
28¼	Godmanchester	9 41	1140	3 28	....	....	9 8	....	....
33	St. Ives 758	9 52	1151	3 44	....	....	9 21	....	....
36¼	Swavesey	9 59	....	....	....	....	j	....	....
38½	Long Stanton 758	10 5	....	....	....	....	j	....	....
41	Oakington D ..|756,	10 11	....	....	....	....	j	....	....
43	Histon .|748, 750 to	10 18	....	....	....	....	j	....	....
47¼	Cambridge 361, arr.	10 27	1212	4 7	....	....	9 48	....	....

Miles.	Up.	Week Days only.							
		mrn	mrn		aft	aft	aft		
	Cambridge ......dep.	7 30	1135	....	2 50	....	4 55	....	....
4¼	Histon	....	....	....	....	....	....	....	....
6¼	Oakington D	....	....	....	....	....	....	....	....
9¼	Long Stanton	....	....	....	....	....	....	....	....
11½	Swavesey	....	....	....	....	....	....	....	....
14¼	St. Ives	7 52	1158	....	3 13	....	5 18	....	....
19½	Godmanchester	8 2	12 7	....	3 23	....	5 28	....	....
20¼	Huntingdon 688, 695	8 7	1212	....	3 28	....	5 33	....	....
22¾	Buckden	8 13	1218	....	3 34	....	5 39	....	....
25½	Grafham	8 21	1226	....	3 42	....	5 48	....	....
30¼	Kimbolton C	8 32	1235	....	3 51	....	5 58	....	....
35½	Raunds	8 42	1245	....	4 1	....	6 8	....	....
38½	Thrapston B 363	8 52	1252	....	4 8	5 35	6 15	....	....
40¾	Twywell	9 1	1257	....	4 13	5 40	6 20	....	....
43	Cranford ....\[547	9 9	1 4	....	4 20	5 47	6 27	....	....
47¼	Kettering 536. arr.	9 19	1 15	....	4 30	5 57	6 36	....	....
119¾	547 London (St. P.) ar.	11n2	3 25	....	7 3	7 57	7 57	....	....
74¼	536 Leicester (L.R.) "	1030	2 42	....	6 4	7 33	7i48	....	....
103	536 Derby .... "	1112	3 27	....	6 56	8 41	8i50	....	....
114¼	604 Birmingham A "	1248	5 25	....	8 43	....	2B0	....	....
164½	536 M'chester (Cen) "	1253	6 25	....	8 45	....	1028	....	....
193	536 Liverpool (Cen) "	2 15	7 15	....	9 31	....	....	....	....

A New Street.
a Departs Liverpool 2 30 and Manchester 3 28 aft. on Saturdays.
B Midland Road; about ¼ mile to Bridge Street Station.
B Via Derby. Arr. at 9 50 aft. on Sats.
b Departs 5 47 aft. on Saturdays.
C Station 2¼ miles from Kimbolton.
D Station for Cottenham (2½ miles).
i Arrives Leicester 8 18 and Derby 8 57 aft. on Saturdays.
j Stops to set down from beyond Huntingdon.
L Except Sunday night.
n Arrives 10 50 mrn. on Saturdays.

September 1925

36. We are looking towards Cambridge again, but this time there is some activity as an evening train to Kettering stands at the platform on 1st September 1954. Bridge No.43 acts as backdrop while a postman loads mail, the station staff observes, and a man sees off a friend. (V.Webster)

37. Kimbolton station closed to passengers on 15th June 1959 and to goods on 28th October 1963. It was sold and by 1986 had been restored as shown here - nice to see the platforms receiving attention, though the extension towards the camera jars somewhat. (A.Mott)

LONG STOW

A signalbox at Long Stow Goods was opened between April 1883 and November 1885, and a replacement box on 11th August 1891. At the time of this 1901 map the facilities were nothing but a short loop / double-ended siding, with signals to guard it, and a weighing machine. In 1941 a bomber airfield was built to the south of the line. Originally for the RAF, it was turned over to the USAAF in September 1942 and the railway provided facilities for the delivery of bombs and ammunition. The site reverted to the RAF after hostilities ceased, but was then abandoned. Demolition began in 1959. Records for 1877-79 show only coal to be received - under 2000 tons annually.

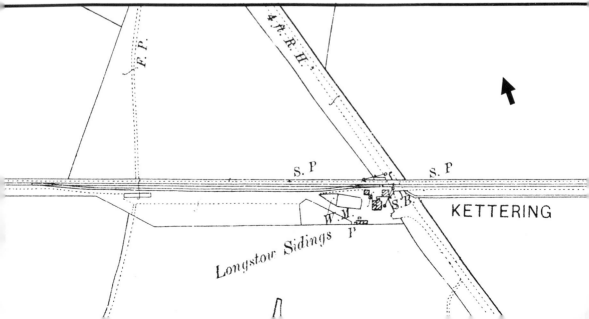

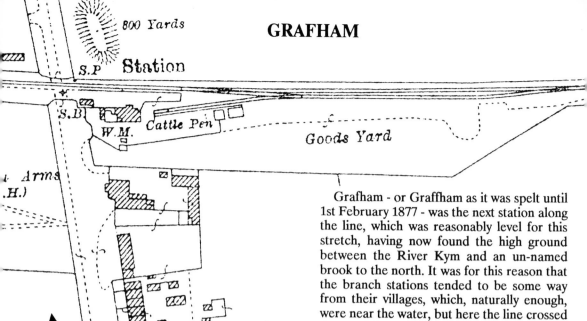

GRAFHAM

800 Yards

S.P. Station

S.B

W.M. Cattle Pen

Goods Yard

. Arms
.H.)

Grafham - or Graffham as it was spelt until
1st February 1877 - was the next station along
the line, which was reasonably level for this
stretch, having now found the high ground
between the River Kym and an un-named
brook to the north. It was for this reason that
the branch stations tended to be some way
from their villages, which, naturally enough,
were near the water, but here the line crossed
the road through the village. The only goods
facilities were a weighing machine and a short
siding with cattle pens beside it.

38. The station opened on the same date as
Kimbolton, and at some point the short
platform, which stood on the south side of the
line, was lengthened. This 1930s view looking
west shows the extended platform, station
house, signalbox on the platform and the level
crossing. (D.Thompson)

39. Grafham station looking east, as ex-MR 0-6-0s nos. 58193 and 58162 pass with a fruit train from the Fens on 16th August 1951. This train, running only during the fruit season, had been known to load up to 70 wagons, which can have been no easy task, even for two engines, to haul up the 1 in 120 from the Ouse valley. (J.Waine)

40. Looking east, but this time after closure, although the track is still down, the abandoned pedal-car somehow adds the touch of conviction that all is over. About this time the track-bed was examined with a view to re-use in a road scheme, which ultimately came to nothing. During the 1870s, passenger bookings rose from 3000 to 4000, but mineral traffic remained steady at under 2000 tons annually. (R.Dorling)

KETTERING, HUNTINGDON, and CAMBRIDGE.—Midland.

Central Station.			Week Days only.						Miles		Week Days only.								

(Timetable columns, times in mrn/aft, with station list including 589 Liverpool, 589 M'chester (Cen), 637 Birmingham§, 589 Derby, 589 Leicester, Kettering, Cranford, Twywell, Thrapston ¶ 472, Raunds, Kimbolton ††, Grafham, Buckden 373, Huntingdon ‡‡ 366, Godmanchester, St. Ives, Swavesey, Long Stanton, Oakington*, Histon 312, 322, Cambridge 310; and reverse direction Cambridge, Histon, Oakington*, Long Stanton, Swavesey, St. Ives, Huntingdon ‡‡ 366, Godmanchester, Grafham, Buckden, Raunds, Thrapston ¶ 472, Twywell, Cranford, Kettering 576, 576 Leicester, 576 Derby, 637 Birmingham§, 576 M'chester (Cen), 576 Liverpool (Cen).)

Notes:
- **B** Arrives at 5 53 aft. on Saturdays.
- **F** Leaves at 10 40 aft. on Sundays.
- **f** Stops on Fridays, also on other days when required to set down from Grafham and East thereof.
- **H** Arrives Manchester (Cen.) 2 38 & Liverpool 3 43 aft. on Saturdays.
- **i** Stops on Tuesdays, and on other days when required to set down from Nottingham and North thereof.
- **J** Except Tuesdays.
- **j** Stops when required to set down from beyond Huntingdon.
- **K** Leaves at 9 35 aft. on Sundays.

L Arrives Manchester (Central) 10 15 and Liverpool 11 15 aft. on Saturdays. N Arrives at 11 45 aft. on Saturdays. P Arrives at 2 30 aft. on Saturdays. Stops when required to take up for Leicester and beyond. T Except Mondays, via Derby. V Leaves at 4 18 aft. on Sats. Y Arrives at 10 18 mrn. on Sats. ...ation for Cottenham (2½ miles). § New Street. †† Station 2½ miles from Kimbolton. ‡‡ G. N. and G. E. Joint Station. ¶ About ½ mile to L. & N. W. Station.

July 1914

41. Grafham station house is here seen from the opposite side. Now restored and extended, it has taken on a new lease of life as the village post office. A water-sport complex is nearby at Grafham Water. (A.Mott)

42. A mile east of Grafham, shortly before milepost 22 (from Kettering Junction), the line crossed a minor road by an overbridge still in situ in 1991. The drop at 1 in 120 into the valley of the River Ouse began shortly after this. The north side of the bridge, which spans the road between Buckden and Grafham, was photographed shortly after line closure, in the company of a Lanchester. (R.Dorling)

43. This picture was taken, looking west, shortly after the line was closed - the telegraph pole on the left is the one on the left of the previous picture. The road behind it leads to Grafham. Thirty years on, the bridge is still there, repainted red, but the rails are long gone, and this view is much obscured by vegetation. (R.Dorling)

BUCKDEN

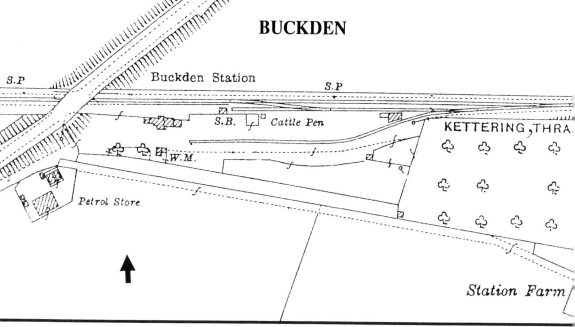

Buckden station was originally called Brampton, and stood about mid-way between the two villages. Given that the GNR had a station on its nearby line which used Buckden in its title, one can only assume that the name change was to avoid confusion with the Brampton near Carlisle. It was not a big station, and this 1927 map shows but one short siding leading off a goods loop, a cattle dock likewise, and a single independent siding.

44. This is Buckden during the early years of the century, with station staff and the lengthmen posed for the photographer on the bridge. The station opened for goods on 21st February 1866 and passengers on 1st March. (Huntingdon Public Records Office)

45. Buckden, seen during the 1950s - the staff is much reduced and the goods yard less full. The building itself shows slight modification at the near end, but the signalbox on the platform, opened before 1884, remained unchanged throughout its life.
(Huntingdon Public Records Office)

46. The signal box was later removed from the site and is now at Fleggburgh, near Great Yarmouth, along with some ex-Nene Valley Railway stock. (A.Mott)

47. Two BR Standard Class 2 Moguls head a 7-coach excursion towards Buckden station during the 1950s - presumably the two engines were in deference to the stiff climbs the train has had to make, coming from the Kettering direction.
(Huntingdon Public Records Office)

48. Buckden is seen just before closure. It is 23rd March 1959, and stationmaster Stan Smith and porters Ted Lymage and Ernie Gibson unload a Kettering-bound train hauled by Ivatt Mogul no. 46444, while the locomotive crew look on. During WWII, locomotives of troop trains with personnel for the nearby camps would pull up to the spot from which this shot was taken (beneath the road bridge) so that the glare of the engine's fire would be shielded from enemy bombers.
(A.E.Bennett)

49. Buckden station closed to both passenger and goods traffic on 15th June 1959, but the signalbox had closed before that, in about 1955. For many years, while the station building was privately owned, it stood unmolested on the platform until it was removed to Fleggburgh Railway Museum, Norfolk for preservation. This view shows the original MR block instruments and trackplan. (A.Mott)

50. In 1955 the station won a special award in BR's Best-Kept station competition. It still looked tidy in 1985, as shown in this picture, but five years later waste-skips behind a straggly hedge made an unlovely sight. (A.Mott)

51. Compare this 1990 picture with picture 47, taken at the same spot - another example of roads taking over. The trackbed is now a slip road from the A1, which crossed the railway (and now the road) by the bridge which can be seen in the background of both pictures. (A.Mott)

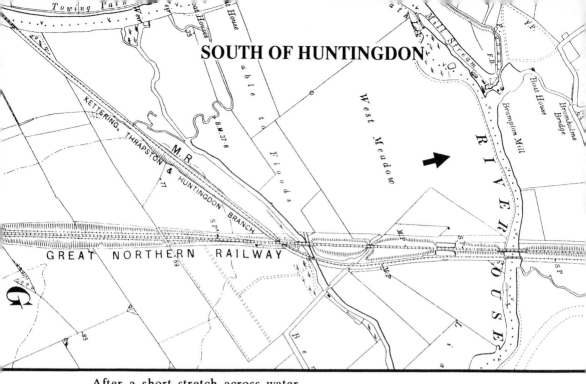

SOUTH OF HUNTINGDON

After a short stretch across water-meadows, the branch soon reached the spur of higher ground by which the GNR main line was approaching the Ouse valley on its way north. The main line, which was there 20 years or so before the Midland attained the spot, bridged the branch, which then swung due north, and, having crossed an arm of the Ouse, headed towards Huntingdon, beyond the right margin of this 6" scale map.

52. Before the line could reach Huntingdon it had to cross the River Ouse, which it did a mile below Buckden by way of a steel girder bridge on steel piers, set at an acute angle to the river. This made a longer bridge, but the alternatives were probably either a higher bridge or a steeper approach. This shot of the solidly-built bridge was taken just after the line's closure. (R.Dorling)

53. Bridge maintenance was a very necessary task and the weed-cutting punt would cast off at regular intervals with divers on board to inspect underwater scour that the eye would not otherwise detect. In this picture a diver is just about to take the plunge. (F.Baker)

54. Bridge repairs on the East Coast Main Line, are seen here in about 1955. One span has been removed, and a connection between up and down lines inserted, with a temporary signalbox beyond. This remained derelict for some time after the repair. Meanwhile, the Kettering to Cambridge line can be seen curving in to cross the river undisturbed on the left. (J.Ellis)

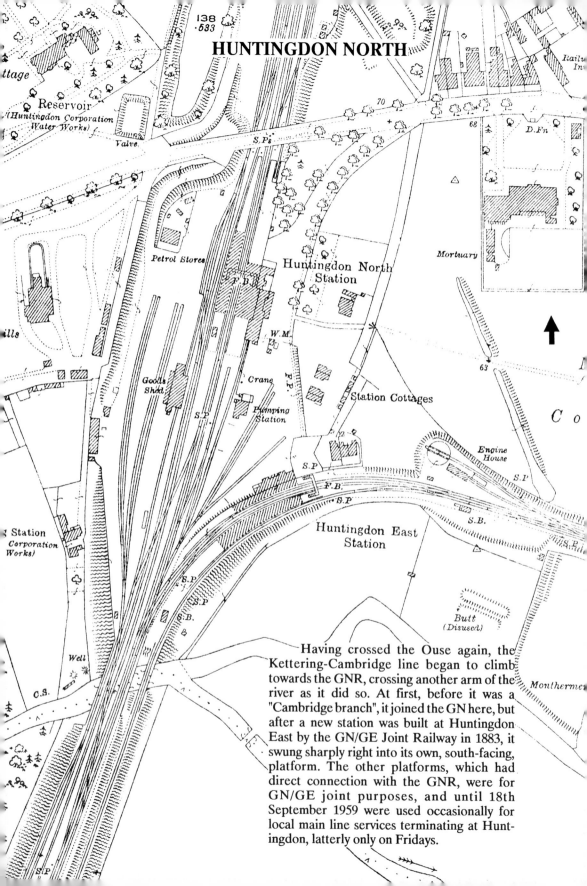

HUNTINGDON NORTH

138
·533

Reservoir
(Huntingdon Corporation
Water Works)

Valve

S.Ps

70

68

D.Fn

Mortuary

Petrol Stores

F.B.

Huntingdon North
Station

W.M.

Goods
Shed

S.P.

Crane

F.P.

Pumping
Station

Station Cottages

S.P.

63

C o

S.P.

F.B.

Engine
House

S.P.

S.P.

S.B.

Station
Corporation
Works)

Huntingdon East
Station

S.B.

S.P.

Butt
(Disused)

S.P.
S.P.
S.B.

Well

C.S.

Montherme

Having crossed the Ouse again, the
Kettering-Cambridge line began to climb
towards the GNR, crossing another arm of the
river as it did so. At first, before it was a
"Cambridge branch", it joined the GN here, but
after a new station was built at Huntingdon
East by the GN/GE Joint Railway in 1883, it
swung sharply right into its own, south-facing,
platform. The other platforms, which had
direct connection with the GNR, were for
GN/GE joint purposes, and until 18th
September 1959 were used occasionally for
local main line services terminating at Huntingdon, latterly only on Fridays.

S.P.

55. As we look south from Huntingdon North, in May 1969, no. 4472 *Flying Scotsman* heads a non-stop run to Edinburgh just before its ill-fated expedition to America. It is already some time since the ECML saw steam haulage, and the once tidy Huntingdon coalheap has degenerated to an almost dangerous extent. (A.Mott)

56. Again we look south from Huntingdon North in 1969. The Cambridge branch ran across beyond the signalbox. Huntingdon has been drastically remodelled in the last 20 years, and the point from which this picture is taken now forms part of a car park. (A.Mott)

57. Days of the Deltics - we look south from Huntingdon on a wet day in 1969 as one of these magnificent machines forges northward with an express. The splendid goods shed on the right has long gone now, but several similar examples can still be seen beside the ECML further south. (A.Mott)

58. An EMU stands at Huntingdon's down platform. It would seem to be going north, but the crowd at the platform end belies this, and the destination blind says Kings Cross. In fact it is the first electric service to leave Huntingdon, the 07.35 to Kings Cross on 3rd November 1986. (A.Mott))

59. A rare bird - no. 89001, not yet named *Avocet*, heads north on 15th July 1988. This was the locomotive's first public run, hauling the 17.35 ex-Kings Cross. The spur on the up slow line leads only into the bay platform, the Cambridge branch having long gone. (A.Mott)

60. By September 1989, Huntingdon was virtually a new station and commuters wait for their electrified service to London, while a new class 91 electric locomotive heads a train of Mark III stock swiftly north. Note that the signal box guarding the entrance to the Cambridge branch has been swept away, along with the goods shed, semaphore signalling and loading gauge. (A.Mott)

HUNTINGDON EAST

61. The GE/GNJR opened a new station at Huntingdon on 1st May 1883, when the line from Godmanchester was extended. It was renamed Huntingdon East on 1st July 1923, and closed completely on 18th September 1959. The Midland had running powers over the Joint line to St.Ives, and this panorama of 1st September 1954 shows Ivatt Mogul no. 46403, in the branch platform with a three-coach Kettering line train. Note the former GE engine shed on the extreme right. The station site is now a car park. (V.Webster)

62. No.46403 has got away at last, out past the double-armed home signal on a concrete post and round to the left on to the branch. (V.Webster)

63. A closer look at the signal cabin - Huntingdon North No. 1 - on 28th August 1954. Note the extended verandah to the left of the cabin for the purpose of exchanging single line tokens. Bridge no. 60, carrying the branch across the river, is visible in this picture too, and note how steeply the branch falls as soon as it has left the platform. (E.Sawford)

64. Hauled by Ivatt Mogul no. 46404, an afternoon train for Cambridge leaves Huntingdon East on 16th July 1954. The normal three-coach set of corridor stock appears to have been strengthened by the addition of a non-corridor carriage at the front. The GE engine shed is just visible on the right. (E.Sawford)

GODMANCHESTER

65. This view of Godmanchester bridge is from Castle Hill. Note the steel span at the left-hand (eastern) end, and the spire of God-manchester church in the left background. The Bridge is on the left of the map below. (E.Denovan coll.)

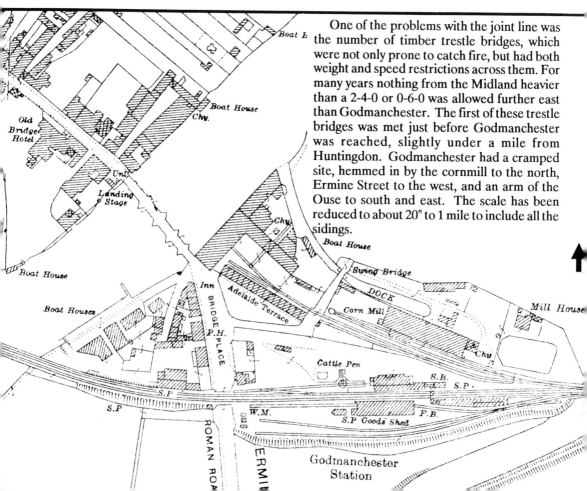

One of the problems with the joint line was the number of timber trestle bridges, which were not only prone to catch fire, but had both weight and speed restrictions across them. For many years nothing from the Midland heavier than a 2-4-0 or 0-6-0 was allowed further east than Godmanchester. The first of these trestle bridges was met just before Godmanchester was reached, slightly under a mile from Huntingdon. Godmanchester had a cramped site, hemmed in by the cornmill to the north, Ermine Street to the west, and an arm of the Ouse to south and east. The scale has been reduced to about 20" to 1 mile to include all the sidings.

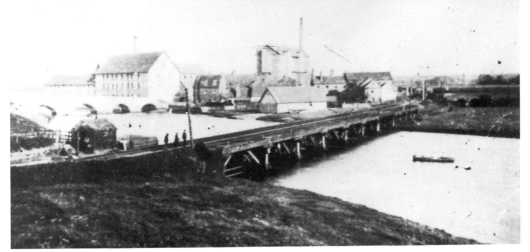

66. The old stone bridge carrying Ermine Street across the Ouse is on the left, and the tall building, rear centre, is a cornmill which was rail-connected. This was demolished in the late 1960s. Godmanchester station is beyond the curve at the far end of the bridge - track on the bridge is still double, and a small gang of platelayers is in attendance. (D.Hufford)

67. The line had been singled by the 1960s, but the steel span of the bridge remained unaltered. Huntingdon's tree-crowned Castle Hill can be seen on the right, the line curving round to the left beneath it. The site of the bridge is now obliterated by the A604 viaduct. (J. Ellis)

68. This magnificent view, taken from an upper floor of the cornmill on 1st May 1908, shows what happens when the Ouse rises. Both Ermine Street and the railway bridge are still just above water level, but both railway company and Huntingdon Corporation must have been growing anxious. Frequent flooding like this on Port Holme, the area beyond the road, caused the racecourse there to be moved to its present site at Brampton in the 1920s. Port Holme was also one of Britain's early airfields. Sopwith Camels and Sea Planes were built in Huntingdon during WWI and some were flown from here although only one sea plane took off from here, rather suprising in view of the frequency of flooding. The west end of Godmanchester station can be seen in the left foreground. When first opened the station was called Huntingdon, which is, in fact, slightly nearer than Godmanchester, and certainly nearer than Huntingdon East. The name was changed when the extension to Huntingdon East opened on 1st May 1883. (Huntingdon Public Records Office).

69. As we look east from Godmanchester station, the cornmill can be seen on the left. Visibility from the signalbox, tucked away on the left beyond the footbridge, cannot have been ideal, and platform facilities look somewhat spartan too. (D.Thompson)

70. Class J15 0-6-0 no. 65457 stands at God-manchester down platform on 10th March 1954 with a pick-up goods for St.Ives. Note the different architectural style of the signalbox from the Midland type we have been accus-tomed to so far: this one seems to show GE influence, as the Joint Railway boxes often had more steeply-pitched roofs. (E.Sawford)

71. This splendid building was once the crossing-keeper's house at Godmanchester (the rear of it can be seen in picture 68, on the right of the railway, beyond the coalyard). The railway crossed Ermine Street at the point where the car on the right is parked - today the Huntingdon bypass makes a crossing of a different sort. (A.Mott)

72. To escape from Godmanchester, the line had to cross an arm of the Ouse again, and in fact crossed either the main river or an arm of it three more times before it approached St.Ives. Although Houghton, Hemingford Abbots and Hemingford Grey were all passed close by, none was given a station. Then, having crossed a road and the river once more, the line ran into St.Ives station, at the south-east corner of the town. Ivatt Mogul no. 46483 approaches the road crossing near St.Ives on a trestle bridge across flood meadows - the river lies beyond the buildings visible in front of the engine. The road is carried on a stone causeway for the same reason. The level crossing, and traffic-lights on the old stone riverbridge, often caused severe traffic congestion. The stately spire beyond the level-crossing belongs to St Ives Free Church. (V.Webster)

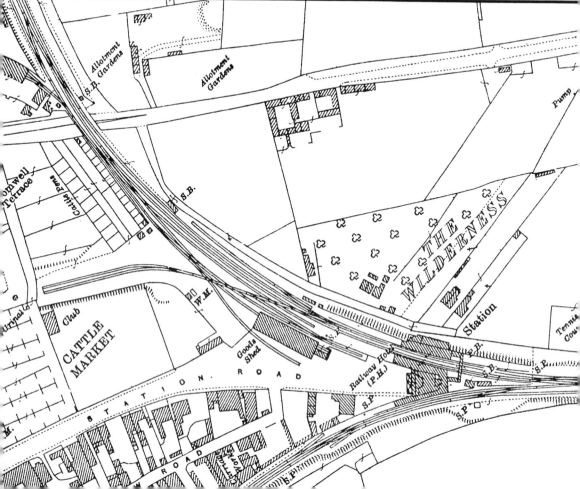

73. Once across the road causeway, and beyond the flooded meadow, a continuation of the trestle viaduct leads to a bridge over the Ouse. The line passed close to the large building with the chimney, where much later, Clive Sinclair began his work on the pocket calculator. A right-hand curve beside the mill brought the line into St.Ives station. (Huntingdon Record Office)

74. St.Ives, on a fine day in the 1950s, looked in better condition before the deterioration of the 1960s set in. The view is of the Huntingdon platform, looking towards Cambridge. Note the prominent water tower, with the signalbox beyond. (Lens of Sutton)

At St.Ives the GN/GE Joint line came in from the north (top left) from March, and goods facilities on that side of the station were quite extensive, including a siding into the cattle market. There were two tracks through the Huntingdon side of the station, but only one platform. East of the station, at St.Ives Junction, the line from Huntingdon joined GER property. This is the 1927 survey.

75. Ivatt Mogul no. 46400, with a train from Kettering pulls away from its station stop, and heads for Cambridge on 27th May 1953. The four Stanier coaches, supplemented by a horse-box, are in the plum and spilt milk livery which was then comparatively new. (E.Sawford)

76. On 1st September 1954, a class J17 0-6-0 makes use of the second road past St.Ives on its way to Huntingdon. A large parcel and various boxes on a trolley await the next passenger train. Note the water column, feeding direct from the water-tower, and the brazier, used to ensure that easterlies off the Fens didn't freeze everything solid. (V.Webster)

77. Class D16/3 4-4-0 no. 62558 takes the March line at St.Ives Junction preparatory to its stop in the platform on 24th July 1955. The engine has been modified with extended smoke-box and round-topped firebox, but retains its pierced splashers. The leading two carriages of what appears to be quite a lengthy train are Gresley non-corridor vehicles, the first a brake/third. (A.E.Bennett)

78. By 1969 the halcyon days were over. The watertower has gone, but not the globe lamp, nor the lattice signal posts. The token is given up as a DMU from Cambridge draws into the Kettering branch platform to terminate. (A.Mott)

79. St.Ives Junction signalbox is seen from the east. The author (CA) has particular memories of the signalbox here, for, at the age of nine and in company with his father, it was the first box he ever visited. It looked much smarter 20 years before this 1969 view! Note the bufferstops at the end of the one-time Kettering line on the left, and the Free Church spire behind the canopy. (A.Mott)

80. Looking east towards Cambridge from the (down) March platform, we note the fine lattice signal-posts controlling both up and down lines, and the shunting signal attached to the footbridge. (A.Mott)

81. In 1969 the facade of St.Ives station had a distinctly forlorn air - the main entrance is bolted, intending passengers for Cambridge being invited through the opening on the right, which led on to the Cambridge/Kettering branch platform. The March platform still boasted a canopy (left) though it had closed on 6th March 1967. Goods services had ceased on 18th April 1966, though the station area was used as a run-round for stone trains up to the late 1970s. (A.Mott)

SWAVESEY

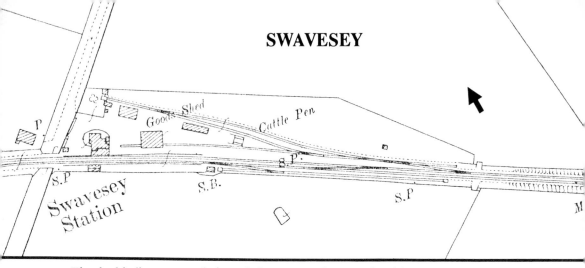

The double line eastwards from St.Ives was singled after services north of St.Ives ceased in 1967. Swavesey was the next station on the route, its station building, unusually, on the north side of the line, away from the village it served, which lay immediately to the south-west. The goods yard shared that side too. On the opposite side there was a short siding, with a safety extension terminating at the signalbox, which separated the buffers from the end of the platform. The present limit of the line is at the ARC gravel pits near Fen Drayton, just under two miles west of Swavesey.

82. Characteristic of many station buildings in GE territory were the long eaves and a rather austere style. By the time this picture was taken in the 1950s, the signalbox - at the end of the right-hand platform - and the siding had gone, though the entrance to the goods yard, opposite, was still in use. One is intrigued by the ladies on the platform, grouped, it seems, beneath a sign which clearly says "Gentlemen". (Lens of Sutton)

83. Renaissance? The line remains open to Swavesey for mineral traffic from gravel-pits beyond the level crossing. On 23rd June 1990, the Railway Development Society organised a special passenger service during the day, to try to prove the need for a service. A Network SouthEast liveried DMU made three round trips along the now singled line, and no doubt brought back memories to many who had once used the line regularly. (A.Mott)

84. Whiteboard and easel were the PA system on that day. A healthy number of people turned out, many of them children, but whether the experiment was effective has yet to be seen. (A.Mott)

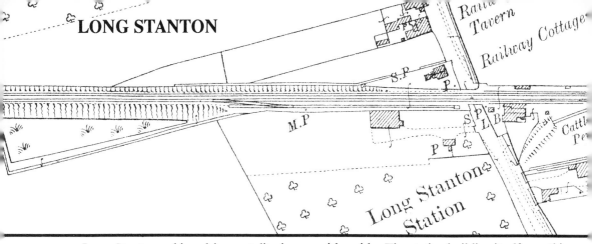

Long Stanton achieved immortality in a song by Flanders and Swann "The Slow Train". The station lay about a mile north of the village from which it was named, and to the east of the level crossing, though there were sidings on either side. The station building itself was, this time, south of the line, the customary rather overlarge house being of similar style to that at Swavesey. This is the 1902 edition.

KETTERING, THRAPSTONE, HUNTINGDON, and CAMBRIDGE.—Midland.

Fares.	From the North, Derby, Leicester, &c., 164 & 165.			1&2 gov	1&2 d	1&2 aft	1&2 gov	Miles	Fm Yarmth, Lowestoft, & Norwich, p.59.	1&2 gov	1&2 mrn	1&2 gov	1&2 aft	
1cl. 2cl. gov		s.d. s.d. s.d.	Kettering.............dep	7 3½	11 5	2 50	7 10	—	Cambridge b ....dep	7 15	1 40	2 20	6 5	☞ No Sunday Trains.
1 0 0	8 0 4½	Cranford	7 50	11 17	....	7 22	4½	Histon b .... ,,	7 25	....	2 30	6 13	b Stop at these Stations when required to set down from Stas. west of Huntingdon only. b Stop at these Stas. when required to take up for Stations west of Huntingdon only. c Stops when required to set down from London. d 3rd clas from Birmingham at 7 55 mrn., Derby at 7 45 mrn., Nottingham at 7 50 mrn., Leicester, St Pancras at 7½ mrn., & Bedford at 9 8 mrn. g 3rd cl. frm these Stas. to all Midland principal Stas
1 3 1 0 0 6½	Twywell c	7 57	c	....	7 29	6½	Oakington b ... ,,	7 29	....	2 35	6 20	
1 9 1 4 0 9	Thrapstone 121	8 7	11 27	3 10	7 3½	9½	Long Stanton b ... ,,	7 35	....	2 42	6 26	
2 2 1 8 1 0	Raunds	8 17	11 37	3 18	7 4¾	11½	Swavesey b .... ,,	7 41	....	2 47	6 32	
3 2 2 4 1 5	Kimbolton	8 29	11 48	3 3½	8 1	14½	St. Ives b ...... ,,	7 49	12 5	2 55	6 40	
4 0 3 0 1 10	Grafham	8 41	11 59	....	8 14	19½	Huntingdon b .... ,,	8 0	12 15	3 5	6 50	
4 6 3 4 2 0½	Buckden	8 47	12 5	....	8 19	23	Buckden .... ,,	8 6	....	3 13	6 58	
5 0 3 9 2 4	Huntgdn n 100, 103 ar	8 55	12 15	3 52	8 27	27	Grafham .... ,,	8 16	....	3 21	7 6	
6 0 4 7 2 8½	St. Ives n 93 .... ,,	9 6	12 36	4 2	8 37	30½	Kimbolton .... ,,	8 29	12 37	3 34	7 19	
6 7 5 1 2 11½	Swavesey n .... ,,	9 13	12 32	....	8 44	35½	Raunds .... ,,	8 40	....	3 45	7 30	
7 3 5 7 3 2	Long Stanton n .... ,,	9 18	12 38	....	8 49	38½	Thrapstone 121 ..	g 9 49	12 52	3 54	7 39	
7 8 5 11 3 4½	Oakington n .... ,,	9 24	12 45	....	8 54	40½	Twywell	8 56	....	4 1	7 46	
8 0 6 3 3 6½	Histon n (86, 101, 120 .. ,,	9 29	12 49	4 20	8 59	43	Cranford	9 3	....	4 8	7 53	
8 6 6 9 3 11	Cambridge n 88, 89, .. ,,	9 43	1 0 4	30	9 10	47½	Kettering 162, 165 n	9 15	1 10	4 20	8 5	

June 1869

85. This view of the up platform at Long Stanton looks west. Note that the signalbox has now been transferred from the Cambridge end of the platform, no doubt to be handier for the level-crossing. A 1950s picture again, but the gas-lamps here have not been "modernised". (Lens of Sutton)

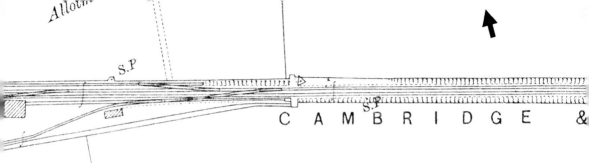

86. The down platform, looking towards Cambridge, a view probably taken on the same day as the last picture. Goods facilities can be seen to either side beyond the bracket signal, and appear to be well used, judging from the rake of vans behind the opposite platform. Only two of the ornate ironwork canopy supports have survived. (Lens of Sutton)

87. On 24th March 1990 the Railway Development Society held its first "special" day on the branch. The weather was not good, and be-draggled passengers await a Swavesey-bound DMU at Long Stanton - here the former up platform is in use. (A.Mott)

OAKINGTON

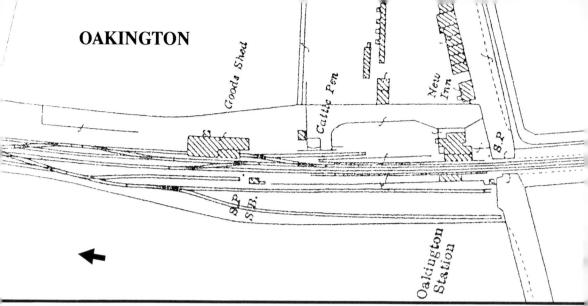

Oakington station stood to the north of its level crossing, its buildings on the up platform. A large goods shed stood on the same side and several sidings on the other. We are now in fruit country and both here and at Long Stanton much was loaded in the season. There was an airfield here during WWII and after, and many service personnel passed through the station gates. Now no longer an airfield, the site belongs to the Army, and as Oakington Barracks is home base for the Royal Highland Fusiliers.

88. This view is towards Cambridge in the 1950s. The substantial station building can be seen to good effect, and a tall lattice post raises the signal-arm well above canopy level for better visibility. (Lens of Sutton)

89. Looking north from Oakington also in the 1950s, this view shows the signalbox and goods shed. Note the canopy-brackets, in a style rather reminiscent of ironwork at Audley End station, and the curious, "chamfered", rear wall. A long rake of vans backs the platform, perhaps indicating that it is the fruit season. (Lens of Sutton)

90. A DMU bound for Cambridge stands at Oakington platform on 24th March 1990. Note the scars on the front of the station building where the canopy once was, and the rather featureless extension obscuring what was once the main entrance to the platform. (A.Mott)

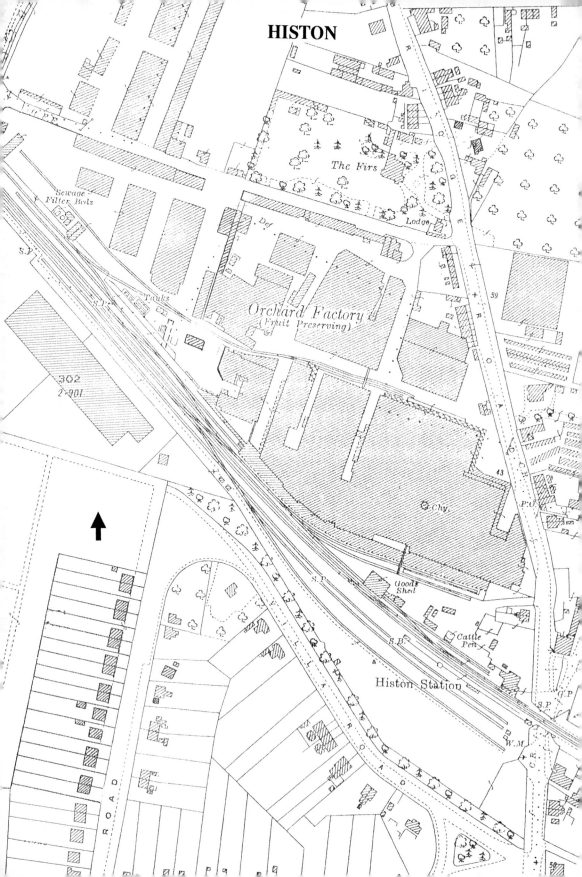

HISTON

The Firs

Lodge

Sewage
Filter Beds

S.P.

Def.

S.P.

Tanks

Orchard Factory
(Fruit Preserving)

302
2·901

Chy.

P.O.

43

39

S.P.

Goods
Shed

S.B.

Cattle
Pens

Histon Station

G.P.

S.P.

W.M.

ROAD

VILLA ROAD

Histon was an important fruit centre, principally because of Chivers' jam factory which occupied sizable premises north of the station, and had private siding and loading facilities. As for the station itself, the layout was similar to Oakington, and the railway had lengthy sidings on the Kettering side of the line, though, oddly, the goods shed was on the factory side. It generated other local business too, when for a while the labels for the jamjars were printed at the "Sinclair" mill in St.Ives, shown in picture 73. The map is the 1927 edition

91. An aerial shot, taken in the 1950s of the factory at Histon, unfortunately did not include all the railway property. Between 1894 and 1898, in/out goods traffic almost doubled, from 10,546 tons to 20,099, 90% of which was fruit. July, August and September were the busiest months, and around 1900 the GE began running a nightly special to Cambridge for distribution to London, the east, and the north via March and Peterborough.
(Cambridge Record Office)

92. Histon station looking towards Cambridge - two horse boxes accompany a van. This 1950s picture includes hanging baskets under the canopy, but plain timber beams support the structure. Again the building is of the standard pattern, identical with Oakington. (Lens of Sutton)

93. The station building looks rather more tatty in 1969 - the hanging baskets are gone, but the gas-globes remain. The signalbox, opposite the goods shed in this view from the Cambridge end of the station, looks small for such an important traffic centre. (A.Mott)

94. By 1990 things had changed. Traffic to the jam factory was no longer railborne, and the station building, though still in use, had little to do with railways. The line to Swavesey passes the up platform, and, now that the station is in commercial use, the canopy at least looks in better shape than it had 21 years before. (A.Mott)

MIDLAND RAILWAY   This Ticket is issued subject to the Regulations & Conditions stated in the Company's Time Tables & Bills.

FIRST CLASS.   FIRST CLASS.
AVAILABLE ON DAY OF ISSUE ONLY.

PETERBORO'(N) to

KETTERING Via Manton

FARE 5s. 5d.   FARE 5s. 5d.

Peterboro'N-Kettering   Peterboro'N-Kettering

95. Mind the gap! Running special trains along lines which normally see only goods traffic, as the Railway Development Society did on 24th March 1990, can present some of the more unusual problems. (A.Mott)

96. This column, beside the line just beyond Histon station, commemorates Mrs Elizabeth Woodcock, lost at this spot in a snow storm while returning from Cambridge market on 2nd February 1799. She was discovered beneath the snow after eight days, "...alive and in possession of all her senses", but died five months later, on 24 July, aged 42. The railway can be seen in the background. (A.Mott)

97. The Railway Development Society was doubtless grateful for better weather on 23rd June 1990 than it had had three months before - see pictures 87, 90 and 95. Here the six-car DMU has just left Histon en route for Cambridge. (A.Mott)

CHESTERTON JUNCTION

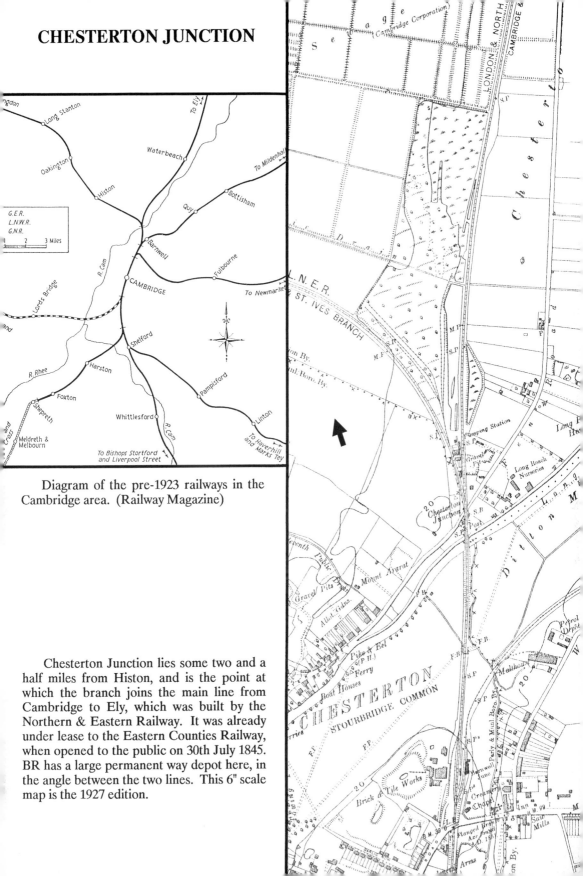

Diagram of the pre-1923 railways in the
Cambridge area. (Railway Magazine)

Chesterton Junction lies some two and a
half miles from Histon, and is the point at
which the branch joins the main line from
Cambridge to Ely, which was built by the
Northern & Eastern Railway. It was already
under lease to the Eastern Counties Railway,
when opened to the public on 30th July 1845.
BR has a large permanent way depot here, in
the angle between the two lines. This 6" scale
map is the 1927 edition.

98. Brush Class 31 diesel no. 31442 is seen at Chesterton Junction on 24th March 1990, heading south towards Cambridge with a parcels train. Standards for the electrification to Kings Lynn have now changed the view from this spot. (A.Mott)

March 1961

Week Days

Miles				Thro' Train Cambridge to Peterboro' (N.)	Through Train Bishop's Stortford (dep 11 21 am) to March (Table 4)	Through Train Bishop's Stortford (dep 1 21 pm) to Peterborough (North) (Table 4)	Through Train Bishop's Stortford (dep 3 21 pm) to Wisbech (Table 4)	Except Saturdays	Saturdays only		Through Train Bishop's Stortford (dep 7 21 pm) to Wisbech (Table 4)	Saturdays only Through Train Cambridge to Wisbech
		am	am	am	am	pm	pm	pm	pm	pm	pm	pm
4	**London** (L'pool St) dep	4 20	..	8 36	10 36	12 36	2 36	3 12	..	4 36	6 36	8 36
8	" (King's C.) "					12S25		3 5	3 5			
		D		D	D	D	D		D	D	D	D
—	**Cambridge.** .. .. dep	6 40	8 10	10 10	12 10	2 10	4 10	5 10	5 10	6 5	8 10	10 30
4½	Histon	6 51	8 19	10 18	12 18	2 18	4 18	5 20	5 20	6 13	8 18	10 38
6¾	Oakington	6 56	8 24	10 23	12 23	..	4 23	5 24	5 24	6 18	8 23	10 43
9¼	Long Stanton	7 2	8 29	10 27	12 27	2 26	4 27	5 29	5 29	6 22	8 27	10 47
11½	Swavesey	7 9	8 34	10 32	12 32	2 30	4 32	5 33	5 33	6 27	8 32	10 52
14¾	**St. Ives**	**7 14**	**8 41**	**10 38**	**12 38**	**2 36**	**4 38**	**5 39**	**5 39**	**6 33**	**8 38**	**10 58**
20¼	Somersham	..	8 51	10 46	12 46	2 44	4 46	..	..	6 41	8 46	11 6
25½	Chatteris	..	9 0	10 53	12 53	2 52	4 53	..	..	6 48	8 53	11 13
29¼	Wimblington	..	9 6	10 59	12 59	..	4 59	..	..	6 54	8 59	11 19
33¾	**March** arr	..	**9 14**	**11 8**	**1 8**	**3 5**	**5 8**	..	..	**7 3**	**9 8**	**11 28**
47¾	35 Peterborough (E.). arr	..	10 13	11 32	1 32	3 25	5 51	..	..	8 41	11S11	1a52
48½	35 Peterborough (N.) "	..	..	11 37	2 25	3 31	5 57	..	..	9 7	..	2a10
41½	38 Wisbech (East) "	..	10 8	11 32	1 32	4 28	5 20	..	..	7 42	9 22	11 42
57	38 King's Lynn "	..	10 40	12 4	2 4	5 1	6 33	..	..	..	..	a1B45

Sundays

	Thro' Train Cambridge to Peterboro' (N.)	Through Train Cambridge to Wisbech	Thro' Train Cambridge to Peterboro' (N.)	Through Train Cambridge to Wisbeck
	am	pm	pm	pm
4 **London** (L'pool St) dep	8 36	2 36	..	8 36
8 " (King's C.) "				
	D	D	D	D
Cambridge. .. .. dep	10 15	4 15	5 0	10 15
Histon	10 23	4 23	..	10 23
Oakington	10 28	4 28	..	10 28
Long Stanton	10 32	4 32	..	10 32
Swavesey	10 37	4 37	..	10 37
St. Ives	**10 43**	**4 43**	**5 22**	**10 43**
Somersham	10 51	4 51	..	10 51
Chatteris	10 58	4 58	5 36	10 58
Wimblington	11 4	5 4	..	11 4
March arr	**11 13**	**5 13**	**5 49**	**11 13**
35 Peterborough (E.). arr	11 43	5 40	6 9	1a52
35 Peterborough (N.) "	11 55	5 54	6 14	2a10
38 Wisbech (East) "	11 37	5 35	..	11 27
38 King's Lynn "	..	..	..	a1B34

D Diesel Train

a am
B Via Ely

c Arr 3 minutes *earlier*
E Except Saturdays

e Arr 5 minutes *earlier*
S Saturdays only

BARNWELL JUNCTION

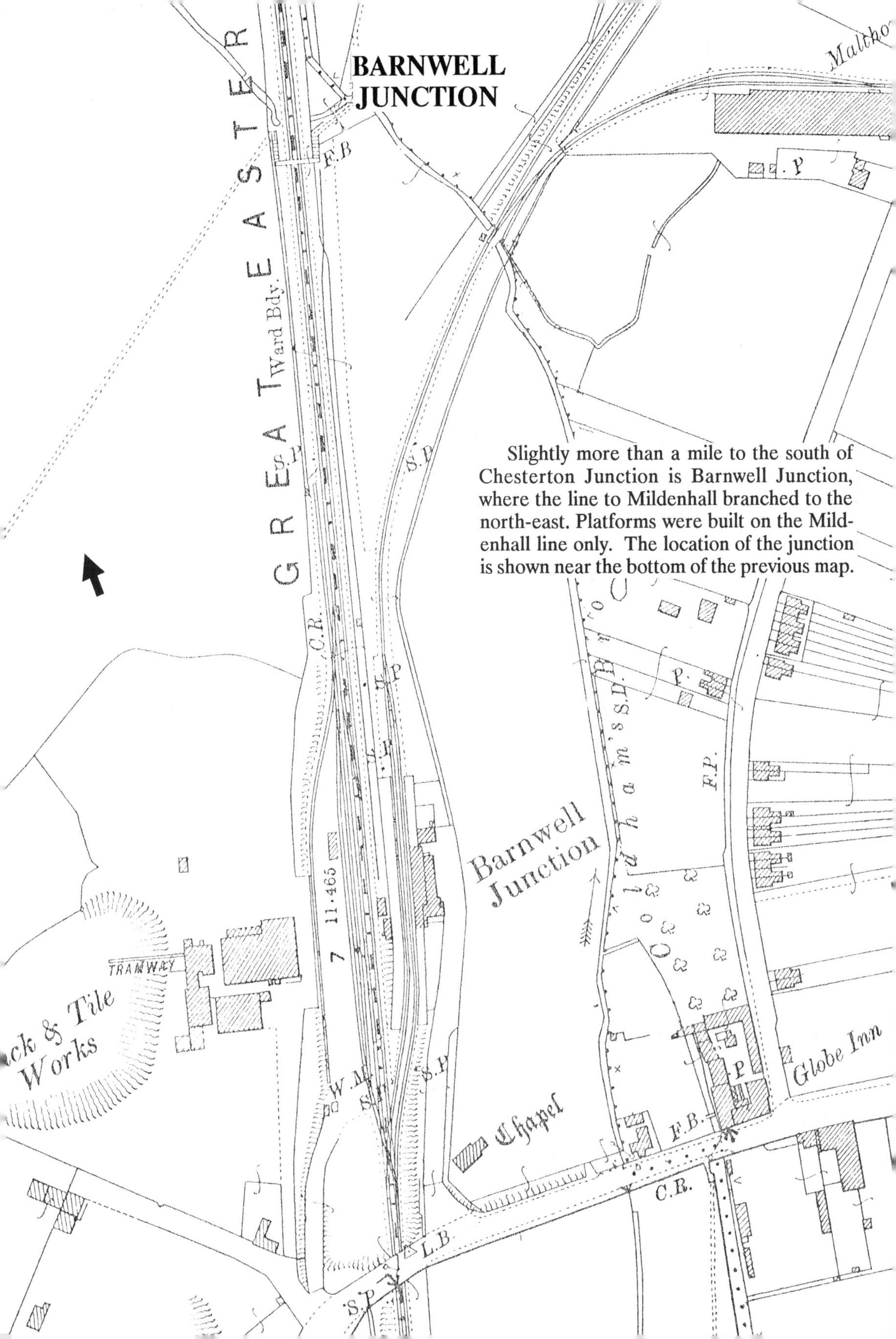

GREAT EASTER

Maltho

F.B

Ward Bdy.

Es.P

S.P.

C.R.

Slightly more than a mile to the south of
Chesterton Junction is Barnwell Junction,
where the line to Mildenhall branched to the
north-east. Platforms were built on the Mildenhall line only. The location of the junction
is shown near the bottom of the previous map.

S.P.

S.P.

P.

F.P.

Barnwell
Junction

7 11.465

ck & Tile
Works

TRAMWAY

W.M.
S.P.

S.P.

P.

Globe Inn

Chapel

F.B.

C.B.

S.P.

L.B.

99. Class E4 2-4-0 no. 62785 pulls into the platform at Barnwell Junction on a February or March day in the early 1950s. The first carriage in what appears to be an elderly articulated set is E63018. In addition to a private siding for Shell-Mex & BP Ltd, there was one for H. A. & D. Taylor. (S.Hall)

100. Cambridge was the last stronghold of the E4 class 2-4-0s. No.62785, now part of the National Collection, but here leaking steam rather alarmingly, takes the line to Mildenhall at Barnwell Junction in the early 1950s. (S.Hall)

101. By 1969 Barnwell Junction had lost its passing loop, though the buildings on the opposite platform remained. The Pullman car shown in the next picture can just be seen beyond the station canopy. (A.Mott)

102. Pullman car no. 156, built in 1923 and originally named *Montana*, is preserved as a private residence near the line at Barnwell Junction, where it was photographed on 24th March 1990. (A.Mott)

103. Some idea of the severity of the curve at Coldham Lane Junction, where the line to Newmarket diverged east, can be gauged from this aerial view, the picture dating from the 1920s. This is the site for a proposed Parkway station, to be served from the A45, and also for a Science Park. Lower right is a coal depot which had two sidings.
(Cambridge Record Office)

104. This rather later aerial view looks south towards Cambridge. Mill Road bridge can be seen in the distance, and beyond it the tracks begin to fan out, right into the former GE depot and left to the holding sidings.
(Cambridge Record Office)

KETTERING, HUNTINGDON, and CAMBRIDGE.

Miles from Kettering	Down.	Week Days only. mrn			mrn	
	Central Station,					
	649 LIVERPOOL ...dep.	..	..	..	7 0	..
	649 M'CHESTER (Cen) "	....	....	....	8 55	....
	649 DERBY .... "	6 15	..	..	1052	..
	688 BIRMINGHAM H "	....	....	....	9 30	....
	649 LEICESTR (L.R.) "	7 53	..	..	1 0	..
	642 LONDON (St. P.) "	4 20	....	....	12 0	....
—	Kettering ....dep.	8 45	..	..	2 10	..
4¼	Cranford	8 55	....	....	2 20	....
7	Twywell	9 0	..	..	2 25	..
9¼	Thrapston D 472...	9 5	....	....	2 30	....
12½	Raunds	9 13	..	..	2 38	..
17¼	Kimbolton F........	9 23	....	....	2 47	....
22¼	Grafham	9 32	..	..	2 56	....
25	Buckden...[810, 821	9 38	....	....	3 2	....
27¼	Huntingdon (East)	9 45	..	..	3 8	..
28¼	Godmanchester	9 50	....	....	3 12	....
33	St. Ives 872.........	9 59	..	..	3 20	..
36¼	Swavesey	....	....	....	....	....
38¼	Long Stanton ...[869	..	..	..	..	..
41	Oakington G...[861,	....	....	....	....	....
43	Histon....[850, 852,	..	..	..	..	..
47¼	Cambridge 469, arr.	10 30	....	....	3 47	....

Miles	Up.	Week Days only. mrn			aft	
	Cambridge ....dep.	1130	..	..	5 10	..
4¼	Histon.............	1139	....	....	5 20	....
6¼	Oakington G........	1144	..	..	5 26	..
9½	Long Stanton	1149	....	....	5 32	....
11¼	Swavesey	1154	..	..	5 38	..
14¼	St. Ives..........[821	12 0	....	....	5 45	....
19½	Godmanchester.[810,	12 9	..	..	5 54	..
20½	Huntingdon (East)	1212	....	....	5 58	....
22¼	Buckden	1219	..	..	6 5	..
25¼	Grafham	1226	....	....	6 12	....
30½	Kimbolton F........	1235	..	..	6 21	..
35¼	Raunds.............	1245	....	....	6 31	....
38¼	Thrapston D 472 ...	1251	..	..	6 37	..
40¼	Twywell............	1256	....	....	6 42	....
43	Cranford........[649	1 2	..	..	6 48	..
47¼	Kettering 642, arr.	1 12	....	....	6 58	....
119¼	649 LONDON (St. P.) arr	4 5	..	..	9 30	..
74¼	642 LEICESTER (L.R.) "	2P37	....	....	7H59	....
103	688 BIRMINGHAM H "	6T2	..	..	9 43	..
114¼	642 DERBY.......... "	3P33	....	....	9 3	....
164¼	642 M'CHESTER (Cen) "	6 52	..	..	11 10	..
193	642 LIVERPOOL (Cen) "	9 16	....	....	....	....

D Midland Rd.

F Station 2¼ miles from Kimbolton.

G Station for Cottenham (2¼ miles).

H New St.

H Arr. 8 3 aft on Sats.

P Arr. Leicester 2 23 and Derby 3 6 aft on Fris. and Sats.

T Arr. 4 15 aft on Sats.

May 1944

CAMBRIDGE

This drawing was published on 2nd August 1845. While the buildings may be fairly represented, the locomotive, with its eccentric chimney, leaves much to be desired. The water column is remote from the single track

February 1890

This Eastern Counties Railway timetable of 1849 shows four through trains between Cambridge and St.Ives on weekdays, with their London connections.   Huntingdon station was later renamed Godmanchester. "Parly" referred to the train demanded by Parliament for the carriage of passengers at a penny per mile.

KETTERING, HUNTINGDON, and CAMBRIDGE.—Midland.

(down)	mrn	mrn	aft	aft	(up)	mrn	mrn	aft	aft	aft
DERBY 265 dep	6 08	8 48	1 17	5 22	Cambridge dp	7 30	1130	2 15	6	5
265 LEICESTER	7 15	9 42	2 8	6 14	Histon	7 39		2 25		
Kettering ....dep	8 35	11 5	3 30	7 12	Oakington	7 45		2 31	b	
Cranford	8 47	1114	3 39	7 21	Long Stanton	7 51		2 38	Sig.	
Twywell	8 53	1123	3 45	7 25	Swavesey	7 57		2 44	b	
Thrapston 205	8 58	1126	3 50	7 33	St. Ives	8 4	1153	2 52	6 28	
Raunds	9 11	1134	4 07	40	Godmanchestr	8 15	12 3	3	6 37	
Kimbolton	9 19	1147	4 97	49	Huntingdon* J	8 20	1212	3	6 40	
Grafham	9 33	1154	4 22	59	Buckden	8 27	...	3 14	6 47	
Buckden	9 40	12 0	4 29	5	Grafham	8 34	Tu.	3 21	6 55	
Hntngdn*154	9 47	12 6	4 35	11	Kimbolton	8 43	1228	3 30	7 5	
Godmanchestr	9 49	12 8	4 38	14	Raunds	8 57	1240	3 42	7 23	
St. Ives 131	10 0	1219	4 50	23	Thrapston 205	9 3	1246	3 48	7 27	
Swavesey	10 8	1227	4 58	31	Twywell	9 13	1254	3 57	7 39	
Long Stanton	1014	1233		37	Cranford [265	9 19	1259	4	7 45	
Oakingtn [132	c	1240	5	44	Kettering 260 ar	9 30	1	9	4 13	7 53
Histon ..[152	c	1240		50	260 LEICESTER arr	1125	2	2 5	29	13
Cambrdge 126	1030	1255	5 20	0	DERBY 260	1232	2	5 86	24	1055

WEEK DAYS / SUNDAYS timetable:

DOWN TRAINS. FROM	mixed morn	mixed morn	Parly. morn	morn	morn	even	even	T even	Exp. even	SUNDAYS even
LONDON	...	...	6 27	8 0	10 57	...		4 5	5 0	1 30
Newmarket	...	...	8 25		12 25			4 25	7 0	5 25
Cambridge	5 40	...	10 15		1 25	...			7 11	5 37
Histou	6 0	...	10 26		1 38	...			7 16	5 42
Oakington	6 20	...	10 32		1 43	...			7 22	5 49
Long Stanton	6 45	...	10 39		1 52	...			7 28	5 55
Swavesey	7 0	...	10 45		2 0	...			7 34	6 4
St. Ives { arrival	7 15	...	10 55		2 10	...			7 34	6 4
St. Ives { departure	7 30	8 25	11 0		2 13	4 25	3 30		7 37	6 7
Huntingdon arr.	7 45	8 40	11 20		2 30	4 40			7 55	6 20
Somersham		...	11 13		2 22		3 45		7 47	6 20
Chatteris		...	11 27		2 35		3 58		8 0	6 32
Wimblington		...	11 36		2 43		4 10		8 10	6 41
March { arriva		Morn.	11 46		2 56	Even.	4 25		8 19	6 50
March { departure		9 50	11 51		3 2	3 35	4 30		8 22	6 55
Peterborough arr.		...	12 30		3 30		8 15		...	7 30
WISBEACH arr.		10 5	12 10		3 20	3 55	4 50		8 40	7 15

(Mondays only noted in the mixed-morning and first evening columns.)

105. Johnson 2-4-0 as LMS no. 20092 simmers while a lineman gets to work. The photograph is undated, but must be prior to 1938, when this locomotive was withdrawn. A Gresley Class K3 Mogul stands behind. (H.C.Casserley)

No fewer than four railway Companies shared Cambridge station. The primary company was the GER, which inherited it from the Eastern Counties, and they were joined in due course by the GNR via Royston, which used a bay platform at the south end. The LNWR then came in from Bedford, using either the same bay or the southern end of the main platform. Finally came the MR from Kettering, and their domain was the bay at the north end, next to the GER locomotive depot. All these companies had their own goods and locomotive facilities, so that Cambridge became a very busy place, far busier in fact, than was apparent from the platform. This 1904 map at 6" to 1 mile shows the original route of the Newmarket branch diverging from the north end of the main platform. In 1896 the junction was moved north to Coldham's Lane, or Coldham Lane in railway terminonolgy.

106. Johnson 2-4-0 no. 21225 leaves the turntable at Cambridge. This class was used for many years on the route to Kettering. (A.G.W.Garraway)

37747

G. E. R.

From   DOWNHAM

TO

GODMANCHESTER.

KETTERING, HUNTINGDON and CAMBRIDGE

Distance from Kettering		Week Days only								Miles		Week Days only							S Y E S	
		a.m S	a.m SY	a.m		a.m E	a.m	p.m					a.m	a.m	p.m	p.m	p.m				
	208 LIVERPOOL (Cen.)..dep	10 10	10.40	10.10		9 30	1.50	2 30			Cambridge ......dep	7 25	11 25	11 11		4 6	4 55	..			
	208 MANCHESTER (Cen.)	12	5 12	5 12		10 25	12 25	1 0		4½	Histon	7 34	11 34	..		5 4½	4 ..	..			
	208 DERBY (Midland)..	5 47	6 18	6 18		12 0	2 52	5 45		6½	Oakington	7 39	11 39	..		5 10	5 10	..			
	227 BIRMINGHAM (N.St.)					11 10	15 3	5 55		9½	Long Stanton	7 44	11 44	..		5 2	5 21	..			
	208 LEICESTER (L.R.)	7 10	7 42	8 14		12 30	4 38	5 46		11½	Swavesey	7 57	11 56	12 35		5 25	5 28	..			
	208 London (St. P.) ..	4 15	4 15	..		12 15	3 15	6 33		14½	St. Ives	7 12	6½	45	5	385	38	..			
	Kettering ....dep	8 0	8 34	9 11	2p10	5 26	6 12		19½	Godmanchester	8 11	12 11	1 49		5 42	5 42	..			
9	Thrapston (Mid. Rd.)..	8 18	8 53	9 29	2 25	4 48	6 27		20½	Huntingdon (East) H..	8 16	12 16	..		5 48	5 48	..			
12	Raunds	8 26	9 1	..	2 36	5 52	..		22½	Buckden	8 23	12 23	..		5 55	5 55	..			
15	Kimbolton	8 36	9 10	..	2 54	6 1	..		30½	Grafham	8 34	12 32	..		6 6	6 6	..			
22	Grafham	8 45	9 18	..	3 6	19 6	57		35½	Kimbolton	8 44	12 42	..		6 16	6 16	..			
26	Buckden	8 51	9 24	..	3 7	6 27	9 5		38½	Raunds	8 54	12 45	2 29		6 22	6 23	..			
27½	Huntingdon (East) H..	8 59	9 24	10	3 10	6 30	9 8		41½	Thrapston (Mid. Rd.)..	9 14	1 5	2 50		6 39	6 42	..			
30	Godmanchester......	9 2	9 44	10 6	3 10	6 41	9 19		47½	Kettering .... arr	11w	63s15	..		8 15	8 38	..			
32½	St. Ives	9 13	9 05	10 16	3 26	..	9 25		74½	208 LEICESTER (L. Rd.)	10w30	1K59	3 32		7 38	7 40	..			
35½	Swavesey	..	..	..	3 31	..	9 39		114	227 BIRMINGHAM (N.St.)	12o57	3o35	5 49		10	9 10	..			
38½	Long Stanton	..	..	..	..	..	9 45		104	208 DERBY (Midland)	124 15	3 X 0	5 0		8 52	9 14	..			
41	Oakington	..	..	..	..	..	9 41		165	208 MANCHESTER (C.)	2 31	4 43	17	2 11	0	11 7	..			
43	Histon	..	..	..	..	..	9 50		199	208 LIVERPOOL (Cen.)	3 27	6 28	9 24	..	..	..	..			
47½	Cambridge .... arr	9 38	10 20	10 41	3 45	7															

b Arr 1 44 pm on Saturdays
c Dep 1 2 pm on Saturdays
d Arr 12 27 pm on Saturdays
E Except Saturdays
g Arr 5 5 pm on Saturdays
h Arr 3 0 pm on Saturdays
J Friday nights
H 100 yards to Huntingdon (North) Eastern Region
K Arr Leicester 1 49 and Derby 3 21 pm on Saturdays
k Arr 4 15 pm on Saturdays
n Dep 11 34 am on Saturdays
p pm
S Saturdays only
u Arr 10 40 am on Saturdays
x Arr 3 27 pm on Saturdays
Y Dep 10 25 pm on Sundays
Y Through Train between Leicester (L. Rd.) and Clacton
w Arr 3 28 pm on Saturdays
Z Arr 9 30 am
† 5 minutes later on Saturdays
§ Stops to set down

September 1957

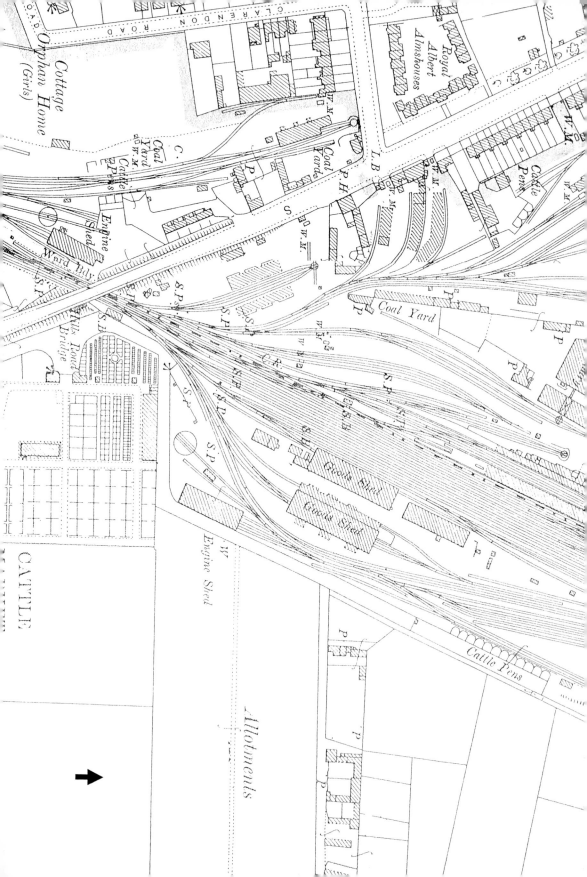

The 1901 survey marks the street tramway terminating outside the station, with the GER locomotive shed to the right of it. The LNWR shed is upper left.

TENISON ROAD

Cabmen's Shelter

Station

Hotel

Engine Shed

C.R. Ward Bdy.

107. Kirtley 2-4-0 as LMS no. 20112 is seen from the former GE loco depot, as it pulls away from Cambridge with a Kettering train, early in WWII. (A.G.W.Garraway)

108. Not quite nationalised. Ivatt Mogul no.6404, barely a year old, stands at the former Midland bay on 15th April 1947, the ex-GE engine shed being in the background. (H.C.Casserley)

109. Our old friend no. 46444 is seen again as the crew receives final instructions before setting off to Kettering, on 7th July 1956. We get a view of the station behind the train here, as well as a glimpse over the wall at Class B1 no. 61371 outside the shed, the site of which is now part of the extensive car park. (H.C.Casserley)

KETTERING, HUNTINGDON, and CAMBRIDGE.—Midland.

Week Days.

Miles from Kettering	Central Station;	ngt	mrn	mrn	mrn	mrn	aft	aft	aft
	523 LIVERPOOL...dep.	11½c0	5 10		9 20	11 5	3 30		3 30
	523 M'CHESTER(Cen)	12c55	7 30		1030	1148	4 20		4 20
	523 BIRMINGHAM§..	4x3	8 12			1135	5 5		5 5
	523 DERBY	5 55	8 52	8 57	1210	1640	5 53		5 58
	523 LEICESTER ..	7 20	9 40	10 5	1 5	2 40	6 43		6 43
—	Kettering ......dep.	8 28	1045	1130	2 4	0	7 20		7 32
4½	Cranford	8 37	1055	1142	2 34	4 14	7 29		7 41
7	Twywell	8 42	11 0	1148	2 39	4 19	7 34		7 46
9½	Thrapston 426.....	8 49	11 7	1153	2 45	4c30	7 40		7 53
12½	Raunds	8 57	1114		2 52	4c37	7 47		8 0
17½	Kimbolton	9 7	1124		3 1	4c47	7 56		8 10
22½	Grafham	9 15	1133		3 9	4c56	8 4		8 23
23	Buckden	9 21	1139		3 15	5 c 3	8 10		8 31
27½	Huntingdon 320	9 27	1145		3 21	5 c 9	8 16		8 39
28½	Godmanchester..	9 30	1148		3 24	5c11	8 19		8 42
33	St. Ives............	9 41	1158		3 33		8 29		8 52
36½	Swavesey	9 49							
38½	Long Stanton	9 55							
41	Oakington.........	10 1							
43	Histon..[278,288	10 7							
47½	Cambridge 276,..	1016	1218		3 54		8 52	9 15	
62½	276 ELY ....arr.	11 8	1 56		4 25			1210	
61¼	287 NEWMARKET..	1132	1250		4 48			1018	
75¾	287 BURY ST.EDMDS	1214	2 58		5 25				
102½	287 IPSWICH..	11 20	4 7		6 29				

Week Days.

Miles from Cambridge		mrn	mrn	mrn	aft	mrn	aft	aft	aft
	287 IPSWICH .....dep			8 38		10 8	1 48			4 35
	287 BURY ST.EDMDS		7 20	1013		1122	3 8			5 37
	287 NEWMARKET..		8 3	1042		1230	3 57			6 15
	278 ELY		8 26	1054		1 7	4 10			6 35
	Cambridge ..dep.		8 55	1118		2 50	4 50			7 20
	Histon............						5			
	Oakington.........									
	Long Stanton									
	Swavesey									
	St. Ives...........		9 16	1138		3 10	5 14			7 40
	Godmanchester..		9 24	1146		3 18	5 22			7 48
	Huntingdon 320		9 28	1149		3 22	5 24			7 50
	Buckden		9 34	1155		Mn.	5 30			7 55
	Grafham		9 40	12 2		Mn.	5 37			8 1
	Kimbolton	8 35	9 48	1210		3 37	5 45			8 9
	Raunds	8 44	9 57	1219		3 46	5 54			8 18
	Thrapston 426....	8 51	10 3	1225	1249	3 53	6 0		6 16	8 24
	Twywell	8 58	u	n	1246	3 59			6 16	8 29
	Cranford	9 5	u	n	1252	4 5			6 22	8 34
	Kettering 512,523 ar	9 15	1020	1240	1 2	4 15	6 17		6 33	8 44
	512 LEICESTER ....arr	10 5	1110	1 52	3 9	5 42	7 17	8 15	9 50
	512 DERBY	1117	1202	3 20	3x52	6 45	8 16	9 33	1147
	512 BIRMINGHAM§	1122	1250	2 18	5 17	7 0	9 45	2 7	2 7
	512 M'CHESTER(Cen)	1240	1 35	3 40	5 15	8 40	9 15	1030	3 10
	512 LIVERPOOL(Cen)	1 40	2 20	4 30	5 50	9 20	1010	1155	5 5

b Leaves at 1 50 aft. on Saturdays.
c Tuesdays only.
d Arrives at 3 15 aft. on Saturdays.
J Stops when required to set down from beyond Huntingdon.
m Stops to take up for beyond Huntingdon.
n Stops when required to take up for North and West of Leicester.
o Leaves at 9 35 aft. on Sundays.
p Except Mondays.
t Arrives at 2 25 aft. on Saturdays.
u Stops on Fridays, also on other days to set down from Grafham and East thereof.
x Except Mondays, via Derby.
§ New Street.
‖ New Station.

July 1906

110. This aerial photograph from the early 1950s gives some idea of the area covered by the railway at Cambridge - and this is only part of it. More lies off to the left, and the former LNWR and GNR both had yards off the right-hand side of the picture. Tenison Road runs across the bottom right of the picture, the yard close by bearing its name. The old GER loco shed is further back and to the left, with the station building to its right. On the far side are the holding sidings, and the former GNR engine shed is at top right. Note the location of the station, on the very edge of the city. (Cambridge Record Office).

KETTERING, HUNTINGDON and CAMBRIDGE

Miles from Kettering		Week Days only				Miles		Week Days only				
		a.m.	a.m a.m p.m E S		p.m			a.m.	a.m	p.m		
208	Liverpool (Cen.) dep	..	9 25 1 30 2 30		..		Cambridge ✷ ... dep	7 35	..	1120	5 0	
208	Manchester (Cen.) "	..	10 25 2 25 4 0		..	4¾	Histon............	7 45	..	1128	5 8	
208	Derby (Midland) "	6 20	12N 0 3 55 5 45		..	6¾	Oakington........	7 48	..	1132	5 13	
227	Birmingham (N Sth	..	1h15 3 15 5 10		..	9¾	Long Stanton ...	7 52	..	1137	5 17	
208	Leicester (L.Rd.) "	7 42	12 50 4 36 6 40		..	11¾	Swavesey........	7 57	..	1142	5 22	
208	London (St. Pan.) "	4 20	12 15 3 15 6 33		..	14¾	St. Ives.........	8 3	..	1148	5 29	
—	Kettering ...... dep	8 25	2p10 5 20 8 10		..	19	Godmanchester....	8 12	..		5 38	
9¼	Thrapston (Mid. Rd.)..	8 44	2 29 5 42 8 2..		..	20½	Huntingdon (East) H ..	8 15	..	1158	5 41	
12¼	Raunds............	8 52	.. 5 52		..	22¼	Buckden.........	..	..	12 3	5 48	
17¼	Kimbolton........	9 1	2 43 6 4 8 42		..	25¼	Grafham.........	..	..	1210	5 54	
22½	Grafham..........	9 8	2 51 6 12 8 50		..	30½	Kimbolton.......	8 30	..	1218	6 3	
25¾	Raunds...........	9 14	.. 6 17 8 55		..	35¼	Raunds..........	..	..	1228	6 13	
27¾	Huntingdon (East) H..	9V42	3 16 2 39 9 1		..	38¾	Thrapston (Mid. Rd.)..	9 48	..	1236	6 20	
28½	Godmanchester.....	9 44	3 36 2 69 9 8		..	47¾	Kettering ...... arr	9 6	..	1255	6 38	
33	St. Ives..........	9 55	3 136 37 9 13		..	110¾	208 London (St. Pan.) arr	114 7	..	3H18	8H27	
36¾	Swavesey.........	..	3 19 .. 9 19		..	74¼	208 Leicester (L.Rd.) "	10427	..	1 48	7 35	
38¾	Long Stanton	..	.. .. 9 24		..	114½	227 Birmingham (N Sth)	12 59	..	3 8	8 58	
41	Oakington.......	..	.. .. 9 28		..	104¾	208 Derby (Midland) "	11P47	..	3 L 0	9 31	
43	Histon...........	..	.. .. 9 34		..	165¼	208 Manchester (Cen) "	2T31	..	4H31	11 57	
47¾	Cambridge ✷ ... arr	10 18	3 37 6 59 9 43		..	199¼	208 Liverpool (Cen.) "	4 15	..	6 28	..	

A	Arr 10 40 am on Saturdays
B	Arr 8 43 pm on Saturdays
E	Except Saturdays
H	100 yards to Huntingdon (North) Eastern Region
H	Arr 3 28 pm on Saturdays
J	Dep 7 35 am on Saturdays
K	Arr 8 21 pm on Saturdays
N	Noon. Dep 12 19 pm on Saturdays
n	Dep 11 35 am on Saturdays
P	pm
R	Arr 1 2 pm on Saturdays
S	Saturdays only
T	Arr 3 0 pm on Saturdays
U	Arr 5 5 pm on Saturdays
V	Arr 9 19 am

✷ See Tables 65 and 208 for alternative service to or from Kettering and beyond, via Bedford. Passengers make their own way between Bedford (St. John's) and Bedford (Midland Road)

May 1959

111. There was an impressive line-up of steam locomotives outside Cambridge ex-GER shed on 18th March 1959, including two "Sandringham" class 4-6-0s. That on the left is no. 61644 *Earlham Hall*, the other to the right of the prominent lamp being unidentifiable, with a very clean-looking J15 0-6-0 beyond. A Gresley class K3 Mogul no. 61835 stands on the road between the "Sandringhams", with another Gresley engine in front of it. (A.E.Bennett)

112. A 1969 view from the north end of the ex-Midland bay at Cambridge shows the diesel engine very much in charge - three Class 31s on the left and a shunter on the right. (A.Mott)

113. In 1969 a passenger service still ran as far as St.Ives, and here a DMU stands in the ex-Kettering bay awaiting departure. Compare this view with picture 109, taken from an almost identical spot. Now the locomotive shed has gone and we can see the granary in all its glory. (A.Mott)

WAITING AND
LADIES ROOMS

114. The Cambridge through platform is seen in 1969, a picture taken before the improvements. The writer can confirm, from personal experience, what a nuisance and hazard all those columns could be! (A.Mott)

115. Diesel 0-6-0 no. 08495, rejoicing in the unofficial name of *Bury*, shunts the oil terminal at Cambridge during the late 1980s. The terminal is due to close when electrification of the line is complete. (A.Mott)

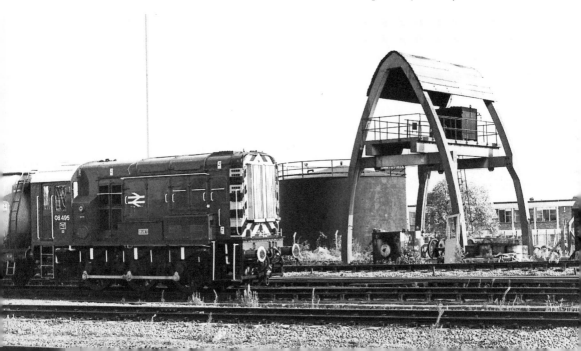

116. New works do have their advantages, for this 22nd March 1990 view is from the new cycle bridge and gives a panorama not available before. Electric wires are up, the shed area is a car park and the station forecourt has been encroached upon by a space-age type building in front of the granary. (A.Mott)

117. 1990 and changes aplenty. The Tenison Road goods yard now has a timber warehouse on it, the loco depot has almost gone and there is no trace of North Box. Mill Road bridge has been rebuilt, possibly in connection with the electrification, which does not yet stretch into the former Kettering bay. (A.Mott)

← 118. But at least the station facade looks well-kept, though remarks about the filling in of the arcades are best left unmade. The Cambridge Colleges were doubtful, indeed difficult, when the railway first came to Cambridge, but by 1990 they had their crests displayed along the frontage. Beyond can be seen one of the suspension pillars of the new cycle bridge. (A.Mott)

← 119. Cambridge always seemed to have more people running for the train than anywhere else, and on 11th May 1990 times hadn't changed. Cambridge has one of the longest platforms in the country, and here we see three trains at it. On the right is the tail of a four coach EMU, bound for London, and just coupling to it is a similar set (317344). Beyond stands an elderly DMU, no. L224, waiting to leave for Ely. (A.Mott)

120. And is this the shape of things to come? A light transit train crosses the bypass viaduct above Huntingdon North station. With much of the trackbed still there, at least between St.Ives and Cambridge, only time will tell. (A.Mott)

MP Middleton Press

Easebourne Lane, Midhurst. West Sussex. GU29 9AZ
(0730) 813169
Write or telephone for our latest booklist

BRANCH LINES

BRANCH LINES TO MIDHURST
BRANCH LINES AROUND MIDHURST
BRANCH LINES TO HORSHAM
BRANCH LINE TO SELSEY
BRANCH LINES TO EAST GRINSTEAD
BRANCH LINES TO ALTON
BRANCH LINE TO HAYLING
BRANCH LINE TO TENTERDEN
BRANCH LINES TO NEWPORT
BRANCH LINES TO TUNBRIDGE WELLS
BRANCH LINE TO SWANAGE
BRANCH LINES TO LONGMOOR
BRANCH LINE TO LYME REGIS
BRANCH LINE TO FAIRFORD
BRANCH LINE TO ALLHALLOWS
BRANCH LINES AROUND ASCOT
BRANCH LINES AROUND WEYMOUTH
BRANCH LINE TO HAWKHURST
BRANCH LINES AROUND EFFINGHAM JN
BRANCH LINE TO MINEHEAD
BRANCH LINE TO SHREWSBURY

SOUTH COAST RAILWAYS

CHICHESTER TO PORTSMOUTH
BRIGHTON TO EASTBOURNE
RYDE TO VENTNOR
EASTBOURNE TO HASTINGS
PORTSMOUTH TO SOUTHAMPTON
HASTINGS TO ASHFORD
SOUTHAMPTON TO BOURNEMOUTH
ASHFORD TO DOVER
BOURNEMOUTH TO WEYMOUTH
DOVER TO RAMSGATE

SOUTHERN MAIN LINES

HAYWARDS HEATH TO SEAFORD
EPSOM TO HORSHAM
CRAWLEY TO LITTLEHAMPTON
THREE BRIDGES TO BRIGHTON
WATERLOO TO WOKING
VICTORIA TO EAST CROYDON
EAST CROYDON TO THREE BRIDGES
WOKING TO SOUTHAMPTON
WATERLOO TO WINDSOR
LONDON BRIDGE TO EAST CROYDON
BASINGSTOKE TO SALISBURY
SITTINGBOURNE TO RAMSGATE

COUNTRY RAILWAY ROUTES

BOURNEMOUTH TO EVERCREECH JN
READING TO GUILDFORD
WOKING TO ALTON
BATH TO EVERCREECH JUNCTION
GUILDFORD TO REDHILL
EAST KENT LIGHT RAILWAY
FAREHAM TO SALISBURY
BURNHAM TO EVERCREECH JUNCTION
REDHILL TO ASHFORD
YEOVIL TO DORCHESTER
ANDOVER TO SOUTHAMPTON

LONDON SUBURBAN RAILWAYS

CHARING CROSS TO DARTFORD
HOLBORN VIADUCT TO LEWISHAM
KINGSTON & HOUNSLOW LOOPS
CRYSTAL PALACE AND CATFORD LOOP

STEAMING THROUGH

STEAMING THROUGH EAST HANTS
STEAMING THROUGH SURREY
STEAMING THROUGH WEST SUSSEX
STEAMING THROUGH THE ISLE OF WIGHT
STEAMING THROUGH WEST HANTS

OTHER RAILWAY BOOKS

GARRAWAY FATHER & SON
LONDON CHATHAM & DOVER RAILWAY
INDUSTRIAL RAILWAYS OF THE S. EAST
WEST SUSSEX RAILWAYS IN THE 1980s
SOUTH EASTERN RAILWAY

OTHER BOOKS

WALKS IN THE WESTERN HIGH WEALD
TILLINGBOURNE BUS STORY

MILITARY DEFENCE OF WEST SUSSEX
BATTLE OVER SUSSEX 1940

SURREY WATERWAYS
KENT AND EAST SUSSEX WATERWAYS
HAMPSHIRE WATERWAYS